100 Days in the Jungle

100 DAYS IN THE JUNGLE

Shawn Ohler and Vicki Hall

KEY PORTER BOOKS

Canadian Cataloguing in Publication Data

Ohler, Shawn
    One hundred days in the jungle

ISBN 1-55263-282-2

1. Hostages – Ecuador – Biography. 2. Hostages – Canada – Biography. 3. Kidnapping – Ecuador. 4. United Pipeline Systems – Employees. I. Hall, Vicki. II. Title.

F3738.2.O44 2000   986.607'4   C00-931502-0

THE CANADA COUNCIL | LE CONSEIL DES ARTS
FOR THE ARTS | DU CANADA
SINCE 1957 | DEPUIS 1957

The publisher gratefully acknowledges the support of the Canada Council for the Arts and the Ontario Arts Council for its publishing program.

We acknowledge the financial support of the Government of Canada through the Book Publishing Industry Development (BPIDP) for our publishing activities.

Key Porter Books
70 The Esplanade
Toronto, Ontario
Canada M5E 1R2

www.keyporter.com

Design: Peter Maher
Electronic formatting: Heidi Palfrey

Printed and bound in Canada

00 01 02 03 04 6 5 4 3 2 1

The authors wish to thank Rod, Jane and Krissy Dunbar; Brant "Barney" Scheelar; Inspector Gord Black; Gar Pardy; David Johnson; David Kilgour; Ken Foster; Anna Porter and Susan Folkins at Key Porter Books; Silvio and Marielos Dobri; *Edmonton Journal* colleagues Nicole Buyse, Candace Elliott, Marta Gold, Randy Mark, Jennifer Parker, Karen Unland and Larry Wong; and *Edmonton Journal* editors Bob Bell, Bob Cox, Murdoch Davis, Allan Mayer, Sheila Pratt and Brian Tucker.

To my wife Marta, who always believed I could,
and my fair-haired boy Joshua, who waited just long enough.
—SHAWN OHLER

To Mom, Dad, Catherine and Jamie
for all the love and memories. Sanderling forever.
—VICKI HALL

CONTENTS

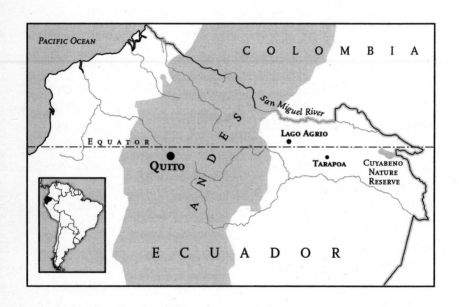

ProLoque

IN HIS RECENT BOOK *News of a Kidnapping*, the Colombian writer Gabriel García Márquez describes his nation as one consumed for the previous twenty years by a "biblical holocaust," an unspeakably violent time of devastation rife with civil warfare, narcotics trafficking, murderous guerrilla insurgencies and thousands of abductions. By the middle of the decade, kidnapping had become an industry in Colombia, worth more than $150 million U.S. to the perpetrators—left-wing guerrilla groups bent on overthrowing the government, right-wing paramilitary organizations that protected the narcotraffickers and opportunistic bandits lured into the game by a kidnap-friendly environment where ransoms were paid quickly and without fuss.

Between the time Márquez wrote his book and the turn of the century, some 7,000 people were taken hostage in Colombia, more than in all the rest of Latin America combined. Ransoms were set as high as several million dollars, and as low as a thousand. Victims ranged from the daughters of political figures to captains of industry to couples holidaying in the nation's lush Andean rainforest. But they all had one thing in common—they were relatively rich, and they had loved ones or business associates willing to buy their freedom.

The left-wing kidnappers, ideologically opposed to the disparities of wealth created by Colombia's oil boom in the 1970s, spent

9

their kidnapping ransoms on weapons to use in their decades-long fight against the government. The right-wing paramilitaries bought weapons to battle the left-wing guerrilla groups and to protect the drug bosses. The guns and turf battles caused enormous bloodshed. Though very few kidnapping victims were killed—it was considered bad for business—Colombia, a nation of 40 million, had 30,000 homicides annually, a murder rate nearly twenty times higher than that of the United States. Colombians became so desensitized to the brutality that in, the late 1990s, television news stations began broadcasting stories about war and violence in black-and-white so viewers would be forced to take notice.

Until the early 1990s, Ecuador, Colombia's southern neighbour, was comparatively placid and quiet, a country with an emphasis on religion that stretched back to the early nineteenth century, when Simon Bolivar liberated the northwestern part of the continent from the Spaniards and formed one country made up of present-day Ecuador, Colombia and Venezuela. Though the areas constituted one nation, each had its own interests and identity—military-minded Venezuela was known as the barracks; Colombia, with its emphasis on intellect and education, was known as the library; and Ecuador, with its preponderance of priests, was known as the church. Bolivar's nation—known as Greater Colombia—soon fell apart, but Ecuador maintained its strong ties to Catholicism.

Ecuador had its share of political instability and military coups through the twentieth century, but, on the whole, remained largely non-violent until the 1990s, when oil exploration exploded, two decades after it had done so in Colombia. Progress, and the inevitable resultant gaps in income and opportunity, brought to Ecuador many of the problems that Colombia had dealt with for twenty years—a rise in homicides and, in the middle of the decade, the beginnings of kidnappings. Crime rates and incidents of irrational violence rose dramatically, especially in the oil-rich jungles of the Ecuadorean provinces along the Colombia border. One province in particular, Sucumbios, which was home to several oil projects belonging to large Canadian energy compa- nies, became known as a popular hangout for vacationing Colombian guerrillas who moved easily back and forth across the border. In 1999, there were almost 200 kidnappings in Ecuador, most of them in Sucumbios province.

In August 1999, several oilfield workers were sent from North America to Ecuador to repair a rusted, leaking pipeline a scant forty kilometres south of the Colombian border. The men, most of them Canadians, knew a little about Colombia's fearsome reputation but were promised that they would be safe on the job. The workers started to fix the steel pipeline in early September of that year, blissfully unaware of the catastrophe that was about to occur—Márquez's holocaust had spread to Ecuador.

The Capture

ROD DUNBAR HUNCHED over two lengths of pipeline, tightening the bolts that held the cracked steel sections together at their broad, flat flanges. Behind lay the dusty gravel highway that cleaved the dense, jade-green Ecuadorean jungle in two, mere metres in front lay the jungle itself, the swaying, ancient rainforest that extends from the edge of the Andean cordillera hundreds of kilometres east to the mighty Amazon River. He straightened to wipe the sweat from his face and squinted into the blazing equatorial sun.

Suddenly, not three metres away, like ferocious apparitions, a camouflaged swarm of men appeared, screaming in Spanish and waving automatic weapons in the air. So strange and silent was their appearance that Rod was unsure at first whether they were real or imaginary.

There were at least fifteen intruders, their dark facepaint and fatigues in stark contrast to the intense sunlight, and they went for Rod's guard first, a tall, solemn Ecuadorean army soldier sitting on the pipeline, looking out for Rod and his partner Leonard Carter, a taciturn young Navajo Indian from Utah, as they worked. Rod knew the camouflaged trespassers were not figments of his imagination when he heard the blows of their fists against the soldier's face. The soldier, in his late teens—a boy, really—had no chance against the menacing horde.

The attackers were quick and merciless. One snatched the young soldier's machine gun, others threw him roughly to the ground, kicked him savagely in the ribs, rolled him onto his back and stripped away his army-issue vest, which concealed an automatic pistol and a dagger. The soldier did not move to fight back. He did not have time.

Though Rod and Leonard saw the fear on the young soldier's strained face, the shock of what was happening did not immediately register with them. As the attackers beat and disarmed the soldier, a furious chain of events that took perhaps ten seconds, the men were so astonished they actually continued to work on the pipeline. Rod was close enough to reach out and touch the interlopers, close enough to see the perspiration beading on their grease-painted faces, but felt oddly detached from the action. In fact, Rod thought he was witnessing an army exercise, that the men who swooped down from the bush were other Ecuadorean soldiers on jungle manoeuvres. He had a fleeting moment to wonder why he hadn't been notified of the exercise.

When the attackers trained their M-16s on him and Leonard, Rod knew this was no exercise, but was for real. The adrenaline surge and the overwhelming fight-or-flight response nearly buckled him at the knees. He was in the clutch of an all-consuming terror.

"Oh, oh, we're in shit now, Rod," Leonard whispered hoarsely.

"Just go along with whatever they want," Rod said back. "Just go along with it."

Rod, grasping for any reason at all why this could be happening, remembered rumours of tourists being robbed nearby. Rod and Leonard were in a rough part of Ecuador, mere kilometres from the lawless frontier of the Colombian border, where people were being jacked for their cars or for their cash.

If this is a robbery, the joke's on you guys. We're working out here. We've got no money, no jewellery, no nothing. You want to rob us? Go for it.

But before he could plead poverty to the attackers, they turned their collective attentions from the subdued soldier to Rod and Leonard, whom they tossed violently to the ground. The assailants took the pipeliners' hard hats and radios and hurled the gear into the jungle behind them. Rod and Leonard were dragged to their feet and frisked, quickly and efficiently. Two attackers prodded them in the backs with machine guns and marched them into the dense bush. Rod stepped over the pipeline and into the jungle, past towering ceiba and palm trees, and through the lush undergrowth of plants and vines. The impact of what was happening began to hit him.

"Ah, this is bad, this is bad," Rod muttered to himself, flinching with every jab from the M-16. Though they had stopped only five metres inside the jungle's edge, they could no longer see the road. The rainforest was so lush and thick it filtered the blistering sunlight into a diffuse haze. The light gave everything a surreal, dream-like quality, as if Rod were in a movie scene shot through a lens smeared thick with Vaseline.

The camouflaged men ordered Rod and Leonard onto their knees, and motioned for them to put their hands on their heads. They spat commands, or maybe epithets, at them in Spanish.

Well, this is it, Rod thought. They're going to kill us. Why else would they march us fifteen feet into the bush and tell us to sit down with our hands up? He thought of every mafioso flick he'd ever seen, scenes in which the mob hoods march their bound, struggling victims into the desert and shoot them execution-style in the head.

As he sat there, an armed, frantic aggressor hovering above him, Rod's heart doubled, perhaps tripled, its pace. The blood drained from his face, and, for the first time since he had arrived in Ecuador, he stopped sweating. His terror became almost palpable, something with mass and density that he could touch and feel in his hands, like the tangled vines and dirt beneath him.

He glanced over at Leonard, but his friend did not return the look. Leonard sat there, shivering and recoiling, as if he expected at any minute to be shot in the face or battered with the butt of a machine gun. "*No espagnol, no espagnol,*" Leonard repeated in a quavering voice.

Dazed and still flushed with adrenaline, Rod's mind flashed back to his family in Edmonton—Jane, his pretty, firebrand wife, and Krissy, their seven-year-old daughter, who had his ginger hair and deep blue eyes. In thirty seconds, three years of memories washed through his mind like a powerful tide. He worried whether he'd told Jane he loved her the last time they spoke. He ached to be with her now, ached to hold Krissy, squirming and giggling, on his lap. He was just an average man, a hard-working, thirty-six-year-old Canadian roughneck, and he didn't belong here, scared witless among the groaning trees a hemisphere away from home.

He was snapped back to reality by one of the attackers, who was snarling at Rod like an enraged wild animal. Spittle flew from his mouth as he screamed; his teeth flashed. The attacker levelled his machine gun at Rod's head and clicked the safety on and off, on and off. The clicks rang out like shots; Rod winced at each one.

It's going to happen, right here, right now. Click. Click. *He's going to shoot me.* Click. Click.

I'm a dead man.

Rod glanced over at Leonard, still quaking with fear, and thought quickly about the other eight men on his pipeline crew. What's happening to them? he thought. Have they been dragged into the bush, too?

His next thought was an utterly selfish one, but Rod couldn't help but hope the other men *had* been captured. Whatever was happening to him right now, Rod didn't want to go through it with just Leonard, with just one other man. He instinctively felt he would need the company of the other men in order to survive whatever his attackers had in store for him.

After what seemed like hours but was in reality only a few seconds, the snarling man hovering over Rod stopped clicking his safety on and off. Rod and Leonard were poked to their feet by the attackers' gun muzzles and marched back to the pipeline. The scene there was chaos.

Several tensed and fierce assailants stood shouting on the gravel highway, stopping traffic and shooting out the tires of cars and trucks so the drivers could not escape with news to Tarapoa or Lago Agrio, the Ecuadorean oil towns at either end of the gravel road. A dump truck filled with huge boulders rumbled down the highway, its gears grinding down and whining. At the attackers' orders, the driver stopped, dumped the rocks in the middle of the road and turned the vehicle sideways, so that it blocked both lanes. Then the men in fatigues blew out the truck's tires.

Rod and Leonard were ordered to sit on the pipeline. At their feet lay more than a dozen of the jungle trespassers' backpacks, heavy ones, maybe 120, 130 pounds each. Just then, two of Rod's Albertan co-workers, Colin Fraser and Brant "Barney" Scheelar, rolled up in their truck. Colin and Barney, both good friends of Rod's for years, were working a kilometre down the gravel road and had driven up the pipeline to see what the commotion was about. The men in camouflage were on their truck like flies on meat.

Both Canadians were hauled from the truck, slammed to the ground and roughly searched. Rod knew Barney, a mammoth former football player, could have crushed the much smaller men with his bare hands, but appeared too terrified to do anything but co-operate. The workers' radios and knives went flying into the bush. The attackers struggled with Colin's work belt—Colin had to show them how to undo it—then tossed it aside, too.

Colin and Barney were dumbstruck, but they still managed to keep their lit cigarettes in their mouths while being manhandled.

"Hey, Barnz, look. I still have my cigarette. Cool," Colin said.

"Hey, me, too," Barney said.

Colin and Barney were directed to sit next to Rod and Leonard. Though Rod's mind flooded with questions, he did not dare look at his friends, let alone speak to them. He realized his wish to be joined by the other men had been granted, but it made him more miserable to know his friends were now in the same terrifying mess.

An attacker ordered the men to pick up some of the backpacks, and marched the four pipeliners back into the jungle, further in this time. As ordered, they knelt on the jungle floor and extended their hands over their heads. An observer stumbling on the scene may have thought the pipeliners were genuflecting to their camouflaged assailants.

As the men sat, fearing the attackers' next violent move, Rod guessed at what his friends were thinking. He knew Leonard would be crippled with worry that the violent men might discover he was an American among Canadians. Rod and Leonard had been on several overseas jobs together, and anti-American sentiment was always rearing its ugly head. Mere miles from the Colombian border, where American operatives had waged war for decades with Colombian druglords, *Yanquis* were not welcome. Rod presumed that Leonard knew it, too.

Barney was probably thinking about his uncle in Alberta, who'd told him about a man who was kidnapped and tortured while on a job in Colombia. Barney had been suspicious and paranoid since the pipeline-repair job started, and Rod knew this assault would petrify him.

As for Colin, Rod could see from the stupid, ear-to-ear grin on his friend's face that the shock of the capture had made him giddy. Colin would be thinking of his wife, Karen, and their three children. Rod's thoughts shifted again to his own wife, Jane, and he wondered if he would ever see her again.

———

On the road, away from the pipeliners' line of sight, the attackers methodically stopped and searched every car. One approaching van in particular seemed to pique their interest, and they stepped in front of it and ordered the passengers out. There were five people inside. Three of them—Montrealer Sabine Roblain, Spaniard Ander Mimenza and Ecuadorean Sonia Falcon—worked in the

Quito office of the Latin American Association for Educational
Radio, or ALER, a non-profit group that broadcast educational
radio programs into remote areas of Ecuador. With the trio was
Ander's sister Maria and her husband, Jesus Magunagoicoechea,
a Spanish couple married just two weeks ago. The five were travelling to the Cuyabeno nature reserve, 600,000 hectares of
undisturbed rainforest, home to freshwater dolphins and anaconda. Several tribes of Indians also inhabited the protected area.
The trip was meant to be an excellent adventure for the radio
workers, and a romantic honeymoon for the newlyweds. Before
the trip, Ander had sent an e-mail message to his mother in
Spain: "We are having a wonderful time . . . We are all going to go
into the Ecuadorean jungle."

The van's five occupants, plus their Ecuadorean driver, were
ordered at gunpoint to grab all their belongings. The attackers
demanded that the tourists' reveal their nationalities. All of them,
including Sabine, a Belgian-born Quebecer fluent in Spanish,
managed to reply despite their terror.

They were marched into the jungle, where they saw Barney,
Colin, Rod and Leonard kneeling on the ground. The camouflaged men guarding the United workers asked Sabine if she
understood English and Spanish. She said she did. The attackers
said a few sentences to Sabine and then ordered her and the other
ecotourists, plus their driver, to kneel beside the pipeliners. They
were ordered to keep silent, or they would be killed.

"What's going on?" Rod dared to whisper to Sabine. "What are
they going to do with us? We don't have any money on us, we
were at work. We've got nothing underneath our coveralls except
underwear. We're not carrying wallets. Are they robbing us?"

Sabine looked back at him, terror etched in her young face.
"No, no, they don't want to rob you," she said in a bare whisper.

"It's something bigger."

A Routine Assignment

IN AUGUST 1999, when Rod received his orders to travel to Ecuador from his Edmonton employer, United Pipeline Systems, he was promised a sweet job, the kind of big-money, no-hassle repair project every pipeliner relishes. They'd be in and out in forty-five days. And, although the job was in northeastern Ecuador, a region plagued by poverty and rising crime, the workers' safety would be paramount. The pipeliners were promised ample security—well-trained, aggressive young soldiers hired from the area's Ecuadorean army base.

Rod was working in Fresno, California, on a lengthy project for Insituform, United's American-based parent company, when he was asked to travel to Ecuador. He was flourishing in Fresno, getting along famously with the other members of his crew and pulling down the kind of lucrative salary that attracts so many young men to the Alberta oilpatch—about $350 Canadian per day plus a $75 U.S. per diem living allowance. Rod was on the job six or seven days a week, a gruelling workload that translated into an annual salary exceeding $120,000.

Apart from the camaraderie and the money, the job was unusually satisfying, as well. He had responsibility; Insituform asked him to rent equipment for the job and he had written cheques for hundreds of thousands of dollars. Californian income taxes were lower than Canadian taxes and the climate was infinitely superior.

It was a heady position to be in, especially considering Rod had never intended to work in the oil industry. Fourteen years before, while working as a manager at an Edmonton Zellers store, his contract had been bought out because of job cutbacks. He'd planned to bum around the Okanagan in British Columbia, but a friend told him of an opening at a small Edmonton start-up oil-patch service company called United Pipeline Systems. Rod met the boss and was offered the job. He took it, almost on a lark, and started work on small jobs in Alberta, never guessing it would be a stepping-stone to a long career fixing pipelines around the world.

Now, nearly a decade-and-a-half later, he was still with United, a self-reliant, experienced foreman who knew all aspects of the job, from welding and operating heavy equipment such as cranes and backhoes to the menial grunt work done in the field. In Alberta, oilpatch workers make better cash than lawyers, and his consistently high salary bought him, Jane and Krissy a big, well-appointed house in Edmonton's west end, across the street from the famous West Edmonton Mall, and an ever-expanding collection of grown-up toys—new Chevy trucks, motorcycles, snowmobiles. Jane often teased Rod that she was the only neighbourhood wife who had to vacuum around new snowmobile parts on her living room floor.

Rod was an Alberta boy, born and raised in Edmonton, but he'd grown to appreciate America, especially its friendlier tax system. He and Jane talked about moving from Edmonton to the States, perhaps to the hilly woods near Salem, Oregon, or to sunny San Diego, so Rod could work for Insituform in the U.S. full-time. They would say goodbye forever to Edmonton's bone-chilling winters.

In late August, though, Rod received a call from Rob Mackie, a United manager in Edmonton. United was under contract to immediately repair an oil pipeline in northeastern Ecuador's Sucumbios province, a petroleum-rich region of the lush rainforest that borders Colombia. But a crew from United's office in Chile wasn't able to do the job, and some other North Americans scheduled to go couldn't either, Mackie told him. United needed to hastily assemble a crew of Canadians and Americans to work on the pipeline. They wanted Rod to fly to Ecuador from Fresno the next day.

Rod didn't want to go; he preferred to stay in Fresno. Insituform was treating him well and had promised to give him money to look for a house in San Diego. Above all, he worried about abandoning the Fresno men in the middle of a job.

But Mackie convinced Rod that Ecuador was a smart move. When the project was over, United would let him write his own ticket. Besides, the job would be easy. Rod and the others were to insert a plastic liner into an eighty-kilometre stretch of aging, leaky steel pipeline owned and operated by City Investing, an Ecuadorean subsidiary of Alberta Energy Company, the Calgary oil giant known as AEC. It was the kind of work the men had done dozens of times before. While in Ecuador, they would stay at a comfortable, City Investing–owned compound near the job site that boasted a swimming pool and tennis courts. Each man would have his own room. Rod would earn the same money he was making in Fresno, plus free room and board. Furthermore, it was an exotic place—a short distance from the equator, and home to unique plants and animals and some of the thickest rainforest in the world.

Rod knew that Colombia was infamous for kidnappings but was less familiar about the situation in Ecuador. He asked Mackie whether the job site was safe, and Mackie reassured him it was, stressing the security arrangement City Investing had with the nearby army base. The pipeliners would be guarded at all times by men with machine guns.

It sounded good. Surely it wasn't a bad idea to help United out of a jam and return to Canada looking good in the company's eyes. He hadn't been back to Edmonton in months, and he and Jane had talked about how nice it would be if he could spend more time at home. Maybe the Ecuador project could lead to a job where he wouldn't have to travel as much.

The job had yet another bonus: Because most of United's American employees were on leave or working on other projects, six other men, all friends of his from Edmonton, would be joining him.

He knew Brant Scheelar best. He and Brant, a hulking, gregarious twenty-three-year-old nicknamed Barney after the belching barfly on *The Simpsons*, had shared some great times back in Alberta. Barney, or Barnz, was about 250 pounds, but babyfaced and whiskerless as a junior-high schoolboy, with a wide grin and a quick, expressive laugh. He was a powerful bear of a man, with massive hands and a linebacker's broad neck, and Rod, a decent scrapper himself, had seen Barney take on and obliterate several even larger guys in bar fights. They both had hair-trigger tempers, especially when they'd had a few beers, and neither was afraid to throw a punch.

But Rod also knew Barney as a thoughtful guy who was close to his family. Rod was the same; he talked a blue streak when he was on the pipeline or in the bar, but was sweet-tempered and quiet around Jane and Krissy. They didn't look like brothers— Rod, with his red hair, narrow eyes and trim, muscled build, had a fox-like appearance—but they shared an easy familiarity, and Rod, thirteen years Barney's senior, treated him with rough affection, like a younger brother.

Rod also knew Colin Fraser and Grant Rankin well. Colin, a dark, goateed Edmontonian in his late twenties, was married and had been with United for seven years. He was relentlessly positive, upbeat, a skilled worker and a constant chatterbox—a good man to have on a crew. Grant, thirty-one, was stocky and good-natured, once an aspiring golf pro who routinely laid down thousands of dollars on blackjack tables and snowmobile equipment.

Barry Meyer, a towering, bespectacled, long-time oil worker in his forties, would be the crew's supervisor. Barry was well-known for being a tough, hard-nosed boss on the job. But Rod knew another side of him, too. In the mid-1990s, the men had owned neighbouring acreages outside Edmonton, and Rod grew to know Barry as a deeply religious man. Barry had three children, and Rod and Jane were close with his wife, Esther.

Two other men rounded out the Canadians. Steven Brent, a shy, grinning twenty-one-year-old, was nicknamed Skunk because he'd once sported a mohawk haircut with a dyed-blond stripe down the middle. Neil Barber, an affable thirty-three-year-old shipper/receiver, would join the men from United's Edmonton office. Neil was excited about the Ecuador job because he'd never worked outside Canada before. A thin, angular man with a shock of dark hair, Neil was the crew's slimmest member, but was strong for his size and a hard worker.

Leonard Carter, a twenty-seven-year-old Navajo Indian from Utah, and Kirk Theige, second-in-command to Barry Meyer, were the lone Americans on the crew. Max Shaw, a young Australian who lived in Calgary, was the tenth United worker.

Rod knew the value of travelling into unfamiliar territory with reliable, good-natured and adaptable men. He was confident he'd have a good time in South America; they'd kick the pipeline's ass and be back home in no time.

In the waning days of August 1999, Rod arrived in Quito, Ecuador's capital, by way of Miami. Quito, a well-preserved colonial city in a high-altitude valley surrounded by the soaring Andes and snow-capped volcanoes, is considered one of South America's urban jewels. Once a major Inca city, it has streets of Spanish-style red-tiled houses and grand plazas and churches. The city's colonial centre was declared a world cultural heritage site by UNESCO in 1978. The climate is often described as perpetual spring, with temperatures rarely straying below fifteen Celsius or above twenty-five Celsius.

Rod, however, had a different impression of the city when he stepped off the plane at Quito's airport, several hours after the scheduled arrival time and in the dead of night. It was abnormally hot, and he found the heat shocking, even after baking the summer away in the central Californian flats surrounding Fresno. Walking onto the tiny airport's tarmac, he was instantly soaked. He thought he was being drenched with water droplets from the plane's engines, only to realize it was just Quito's steamy humidity. As the clock approached midnight, the temperature was still in the high twenties. Rod frowned at the thought of grappling with pipe in these temperatures, let alone the heat of midday.

He'd heard that Ecuador was a poor country, but as he approached the terminal he was alarmed by what he saw. Thousands of people stood crammed together behind a three-metre-high chain-link fence staring at Rod and the other North Americans as they crossed the tarmac.

Inside the terminal, Rod watched as hundreds more locals manoeuvred to try to carry his and his fellow passengers' luggage. He felt dozens of hands on his back, his bag, his hips. An airport security guard waded through the crowd, beating at the obviously destitute locals with a stick. Everywhere, a sense of overwhelming, desperate chaos hung in the air.

Rod had done jobs all over the world—in Scotland, in Ghana, throughout the U.S.—but had never witnessed a scene like this. Ghana was poor, yes, but Ecuador seemed much more aggressively so. The scene was unnerving. He hoped Rob Mackie's promise of security on the job site would prove true.

Later that night, lying in bed in a City Investing–owned apartment building in the heart of Quito, Rod heard gunshots, then the sounds of squealing tires and chilling screams. What was he getting himself into?

———————

Ecuador's political, economic and social situation is as complex and fraught with problems as that of any country in Latin America.

A country of twelve million, bordered by Colombia to the north and Peru to the south, Ecuador has abundant natural resources—petroleum, forests, minerals, fish, coffee, cocoa, bananas. Experts claim that if those resources were fully developed, Ecuador would be as rich as Switzerland. Yet the country is impoverished, with huge disparities in income that have created an enormous lower class. In fact, although Ecuador's economy has improved steadily since the late 1980s, when petroleum exploration began to boom, the nation ranks among the poorest in South America. Its currency, the *sucre*, is devalued, inflation is high, and the government is saddled with a $13-billion debt. Political tension, stemming from the days of the Spanish conquest, exists between a minority of affluent landholders of European descent and the majority of poorer indigenous or part-Indian peoples. To compound problems, international observers rank Ecuador in the top ten of the world's most corrupt democracies. The government has been plagued by scandal. In 1995, the vice-president resigned after being accused of depositing state funds into private bank accounts.

United Pipeline's job was in the heart of Ecuador's Oriente region, 250 kilometres from Quito in a massive area of tropical rainforest east of the Andean divide. Although the Amazon River doesn't flow through Ecuador, the Oriente, which literally means the Orient, or east in Spanish, is considered part of the upper Amazon basin because its streams eventually empty into the famous South American river. Some parts of the Oriente basin receive fifteen metres of rain each year, compared to a half metre yearly precipitation in Edmonton.

Before the petroleum industry moved into Ecuador and began razing rainforest to make way for roads and work camps, the Oriente was untouched jungle, home to indigenous peoples virtually unaffected by the encroachment of industry and development. Farmers, many displaced from major urban centres such as Quito and the coastal city of Guayaquil, have since followed the oilmen to the area, slashing away tracts of the jungle and turning the newly barren ground into pasture for their cattle. Still, although the Oriente is now inhabited and acres of rainforest are lost to slash-and-burn farmers and petroleum speculators each day, huge tracts remain wild and untouched.

The United workers were to fix a badly corroded pipeline that paralleled the bumpy, dusty gravel highway between the oil towns of Lago Agrio and Tarapoa. AEC, the pipeline's owner, had committed millions of dollars to bring its stake of the petroleum infrastructure up to Canadian standards. With production of 40,000 barrels a day, it was the largest Canadian player in the country, drawn to Ecuador by its rich crude reserves and the Ecuadorean government's fervent desire to lure international investment. The work United was hired to do was a relatively small but important part of AEC's reconstruction. Once the project was finished, the pipeline would return to use, pumping heavy crude to Lago Agrio, where it joined a massive pipeline that stretched all the way to the Pacific seaport of Esmeraldas.

For the duration of the job, the United workers were to stay at a City Investing–owned compound near Tarapoa, a grimy, little jungle town, with perhaps a few hundred people living in tin-roofed shacks on dirt streets. Tarapoa is only forty kilometres from Colombia's southern border, a violent area infamous for bands of marauding bandits, controlled by the Revolutionary Armed Forces of Colombia, known by its Spanish acronym, FARC, a Marxist guerrilla group responsible for the lion's share of Colombia's kidnappings. In recent years, criminals have leaked south across the border into the Oriente, bringing with them a rise in robberies, muggings, narcotics trafficking and violent assaults. Some fifty kilometres west of Tarapoa, even closer to the Colombian border, is Lago Agrio, a town of 20,000 and the capital of Ecuador's Sucumbios province. Lago Agrio, named by

Texaco workers after a Texan oil town called Sour Lake, was rumoured to be a favoured haunt for vacationing FARC members. Pictures of wanted men and women paper its post office walls.

The City Investing compound, known locally as The Block, is a veritable luxury resort compared to the surrounding area. It has a paved landing strip, long and wide enough to land a Hercules transport plane, landscaped grounds, a swimming pool, tennis courts and a weight room. Most importantly, it is fenced and guarded twenty-four hours a day by heavily armed security men. The Block appears an oasis of normalcy and security in a land where unpredictability and violence are the norm.

The morning after hearing the gunshots and screams from his Quito apartment, Rod boarded a chartered plane and flew to The Block's private airstrip. As he flew over the Oriente, he marvelled at the lush jungle canopy spread out below him. Rolling hills of dark green foliage extended in every direction as far as the eye can see, thicker and wilder than any Alberta bush.

As soon as he landed at The Block, Rod was warned not to venture anywhere outside the compound's gates after dark. If he needed cigarettes or toiletries or extra food, local security guards would venture into town to fetch them. Above all, Rod was to avoid the brothels in Tarapoa. Sometimes, five or six of the prostitutes would sit on a bench in front of The Block's front gate, hoping to attract business from the North American workers.

The Block's doctor gave Rod a crude warning about the prostitutes. Pointing to a dirty, sewage-filled stream bisecting The Block's property he said: "If you have the urge, stick your dick in that stream, because you'll get fewer diseases from that than from any woman around here."

Rod told the doctor he didn't have to worry; he was here to work, not to screw around.

After a quick tour of The Block, Rod met Barry Meyer, who was already in Ecuador preparing the job site. His other fellow co-workers arrived in the following days. Like old friends, they greeted each other confidently, with swagger in their steps, and all made light of the tight security and grim poverty—all, that is, except for Brant "Barney" Scheelar.

The appalling conditions in Tarapoa immediately confirmed Barney's worst apprehensions. Barney had worked for United in the mid-1990s, taken a leave and rejoined the company only three days before the Ecuador trip. Before flying to Quito and then to The Block, he'd fretted about the dangers he might face in South America. His uncle had worked in Colombia in the mid-1990s and knew an Italian man who'd been kidnapped and tortured there by an unidentified guerrilla group. The Italian worker survived, but the uncle filled Barney's head with warnings and fears.

Before he left, during his final visit to United's office in Edmonton, Barney tried to laugh off his misgivings.

"I sure hope we don't get kidnapped down there," he told one of the women at the office.

"Barney," she said, "if you get taken, we're going to pay them to keep you."

The joking was a defense mechanism, and a poor one at that. It did nothing to calm Barney's misgivings about the trip.

Then, as he drove to catch the first of his planes from Edmonton to Quito, something happened—a coincidence, a fluke, a genuine premonition. Whatever it was, it scared him to death.

Barney and his girlfriend Crystal were rushing from Barney's home in Sherwood Park, an Edmonton suburb, to the airport forty-five minutes away when he suddenly realized he needed to give Crystal some cash to pay bills while he was away. He pulled into a 7-11 to withdraw some money from the bank machine.

At that very moment, an entire city block lost power. Streetlights snuffed out like candles. Two minutes later, with Barney still spooked by the electricity outage, the song "I'm Leaving on a Jet Plane" came on the radio. When he heard the lyric, "Don't know when I'll be back again," Barney shuddered. He was not a superstitious man, but the lyric seemed charged with new meaning.

Is this the smartest thing to be doing? he thought. Maybe I should turn around right now and go back home.

He thought he was hiding his fear from Crystal, but when she dropped him off at the airport, she started crying. Barney said a quick goodbye, so he could leave before betraying the reasons for his skittishness. He didn't want to frighten her.

When he arrived at Quito's airport, hours later, dozens of Ecuadoreans accosted him, begging for money or the chance to carry his bags. A six-year-old boy, perhaps one-fifth Barney's size, grabbed the Canadian's leg as he walked past, hoisted Barney's new Kodiak boot onto a rickety stool and began spit-shining it.

I am definitely not in Canada anymore, Barney thought.

Arriving at The Block, he mentioned his uncle's concerns to the other men, but they chided him for being a pessimist and a worrywart. Colin had researched Ecuador on the Internet with his kids, and reassured Barney there was nothing to worry about. Colombia was dangerous, sure. But this wasn't Colombia.

On September 1, with all the United workers assembled at The Block, the work began. In the morning, the ten United workers, aided by about a dozen Ecuadoreans hired by City Investing, were split into a half-dozen groups of three or four men each. The men were to repair the eighty-kilometre pipeline two clicks at a time. It was methodical, back-breaking work. One group of workers split the pipeline apart at its flanges, where it was held together by sixteen thick bolts. Another crew fused together thirteen-metre lengths of plastic liner into much longer lengths, with the aid of machines that generate intense heat. Once these liners were inserted, creating a new, leak-proof pipeline inside the old, cracked steel, another group would bolt the steel flanges back together.

As Rob Mackie had promised Rod, four Ecuadorean army soldiers in fatigues, armed with M-16 machine guns, guarded the pipeliners as they worked. Rod was pleased with the security arrangements and the project's demands. He was paired with Leonard; the two were in charge of wrestling the repaired pipeline sections back together and replacing the bolts, finger-tight.

The first day on the job was sweltering, well into the forties under a blazing sun. Rod had never experienced heat like this, neither in Ghana nor the numerous oil-rich areas in the southern American panhandle where he'd worked. The jungle towered above, mere metres from both sides of the gravel Lago Agrio–Tarapoa highway, yet offered no shade or respite from the stultifying temperatures. If anything, the foliage, split by the crudely cut roadway, seemed only to trap the heat.

The pipeliners, larger and less acclimatized to the temperature than their Ecuadorean helpers, downed gallons of water and liquid electrolytes to keep up their strength. The men would stop after ten or fifteen minutes of intense work to fight off dizziness. Dust kicked up from buses and trucks crawling down the gravel road aggravated the situation. Often, Rod and Leonard worked with Barney and Colin, and Rod watched as Barney, an asthmatic, took puffs from his inhaler to fight his wheezing.

Still, the United crew made good time. Lunch came out from the camp in trucks, so they took only short breaks. The pipeline was almost all above ground, so there was little digging or anchoring involved. The workers were able to take shortcuts and moved quickly down the road. Even when their air compressors broke down, the men forged ahead, bolting the steel pipeline's flanges together with a sledgehammer and a hammer wrench.

Oil patch work is neither gentle nor refined. The men smoked, swore and ribbed each other constantly. "Put your purse down and swing that sledge, Barnz," a grinning Rod said to Barney, his blue eyes crinkling and narrowing into devilish slits. "Get your fucking back into it!" Morale was high.

The workers got along well with the hired locals and the soldiers assigned to guard them. The Ecuadoreans marvelled at Barney's size as he hoisted tiny local workers by the backs of their coveralls and moved them when they were in the way. They called Barney "Gordo"—Spanish for giant. Although the two sides had difficulties communicating at first, with each passing day the locals learned more English and the United men more Spanish. Rod showed a facility for the language, quickly picking up several useful conversational phrases, such as *"Qué hora es?"* ("What time is it?").

After each twelve-hour shift, the United workers drove back to The Block and took a dip in the compound's pool. The cool water was nirvana after the grime and heat on the line. Later, some of the men signed out mountain bikes and cruised up and down the smooth runway. Others, as if they hadn't expended enough energy during the day, pumped iron in the weight room. They hung out and ate huge meals in The Block's cafeteria.

Gradually, they fell into a post-shift routine, doing whatever they could to stay out of their rooms. The sleeping quarters, unlike the rest of The Block's amenities, were not as advertised, being little more than Sea Rail crates divided into two. And, instead of one man per room, the arrangement was two to a room.

Even worse, Rod's bathroom was infested with tiny, biting insects that feasted on his ankles when he used the toilet, leaving dozens of itchy red dots. As the days passed, the bites moved up his legs to his crotch and stomach. He was given cream and alcohol by The Block's physician.

Rod thought he had it bad until Neil Barber showed off his room.

"Do your bugs look like these bugs?" Neil asked Rod, lifting up his toilet seat.

"Errrggh! No, my bugs do NOT look like that," Rod said.

Thousands of infinitesimal red mites crawled on the porcelain and the fixtures, swarming in a gelatinous mass.

"How can you even put your ass on that seat, Neil?" Rod said. "That is disgusting."

More problems with the camp gradually emerged. One day, the compound's sewer quit working and the men had to pad out of their rooms to use the lone functional toilet by the pool. Then the satellite phone, the Canadians' only link with the outside world, went down for hours, even days, at a time. Rod worried about what would happen if someone were injured on the line. Would they have to drive all the way to Lago Agrio to use a phone, caught behind an overflowing bus crawling along at forty kilometres per hour? What if someone cut off his arm, or was caught under a backhoe? Who would call the airplane to evacuate them? A man could easily bleed to death in the time it would take to summon help.

Rod, who relied on his strength to earn his livelihood, could imagine only physical loss: an arm, a leg, perhaps a wallet. The thought that they might lose something more—their freedom—occurred only to Barney.

It was only a matter of time until the frustrations carried over to the job site. As the early September days passed, the "shit equipment," as Rod called it, was starting to slow them down. They were in danger of slipping behind schedule, and though they were only a half-dozen days in, guys were already itching to get the job over with. Rod and some of the others thought they needed more trucks, in case there were accidents. Everyone agreed they needed more security.

Though the pipeliners had four military guards, two were often away from the job site, travelling with either Barry Meyer or Kirk Theige back and forth from Lago Agrio for supplies and equipment. Colin and Barney, who were paired up, hardly ever had a military escort and were not pleased. The men grumbled that changes were needed, and needed now.

On September 7, about a week into the job, the crew moved down the pipeline toward Lago Agrio and into increasingly dangerous territory. Rod noticed that the Ecuadorean helpers were acting strangely. Late in the afternoon, as the sun dipped behind the trees, the locals tucked their gold chains into their coveralls, yanked their hats down over their ears and pulled their bandanas up to cover their faces. They were obviously scared of being robbed.

Rod also noticed a change in the passengers on the buses that rumbled past the pipeline. At the beginning of the month, they hung out the bus windows, smiling and waving to the foreign pipeliners. Now, they were screaming angrily and shaking their fists.

More disquieting were rumours that tourists had been robbed just fifteen kilometres away from The Block. Security at the compound warned the men again not to linger at the job site after dark.

But the most frightening harbinger that something was wrong came on September 9.

At noon that day, Barney collapsed with heat exhaustion and spent the rest of the day downing litres of water and electrolytes. Then, out of the blue, two locals who worked with Rod told him something that chilled him to the bone.

In a mix of Spanish and English, one said he'd recently returned from vacation in Colombia and heard that in two or three days, something was going to happen to the Canadians as they moved further towards Lago Agrio. He didn't say how he knew, but he seemed certain.

"Maybe rob, maybe kill," said the other local, his English fractured but the menace in his message clear.

Rod didn't know what to think. Maybe the locals were paranoid, or pulling a joke. But the warning did seem to fit in with their recent behaviour. Rod spread the word to his co-workers, and Colin, who also felt something was wrong, said they should demand a meeting with Kirk and Barry when the crew returned to The Block at the end of their shift.

Kirk and Barry agreed and a meeting was set for 7 p.m. in the compound's boardroom. Before it convened, Rod talked to Leonard, who also had experience working all over the world.

"Leonard, man, out of all the places we've ever gone, I have a really bad feeling about this place," Rod said.

"Me, too," said Leonard.

The meeting went well, considering there was little that could be done immediately. Colin, Rod and the other workers spoke about the disturbing things they'd seen and heard on the line, and demanded more armed security and more vehicles. Barry and Kirk, a safety boss from United's office in Durango, Colorado, agreed. They would make the calls in the morning. But because Tarapoa was so isolated—at least a ten-hour drive from Quito—it would take time. In the meantime, they would have to be patient and professional and carry on with the project.

After the meeting, Rod called Jane on the satellite phone, which, mercifully, was working again.

He tried to hide his fear from Jane, but his wife knew him too well.

"What's the matter?" she finally insisted after a few minutes of small talk. "No more talking in code."

"I don't know," he said.

"What do you mean, you don't know?"

"Something's the matter," Rod said. "I just wish I could come home."

Only once before had he felt in danger on the job, while working on a Ghanaian hydro plant which supplied electricity to Western-owned gold and diamond mines. Arab terrorists threatened to blow up the plant if they discovered Americans working there.

Rod listened as Jane pleaded with him. If you want to, come home, she said.

But he could never abandon the other guys or the company. It was a matter of pride, and a practical problem. If he came home now, in the middle of a project, he would probably be fired. He and Jane could forget Oregon or San Diego; they could forget about settling down.

The next morning, September 10, the United workers' armed security contingent was boosted from four to six, presumably with reinforcements from the nearby military base in Lago Agrio. Some non-military security men armed with machetes also joined the group, and mostly directed traffic on the road.

Rod, still mindful of his unnerving conversation with the Ecuadorean helpers, felt a bit more secure with the added manpower. He and the others plugged away on the line and finished the day with twenty-three kilometres of pipe fixed, more than a quarter of the job complete. Despite their problems—the security, the "shit equipment," the stifling climate—they were on schedule, if not ahead.

September 11 dawned hot and clear. For unexplained reasons, the pipeliners' military security force was cut back from six to four, but Rod assumed it was an anomaly, that more soldiers would be added to protect them.

Partners Rod and Leonard were dropped off at their point on the job site, about 800 metres down the road from Colin and Barney. Rod hopped out of the truck, beads of sweat forming instantly on his neck and arms. He, Leonard and the other guys had taken to wearing coveralls with only their underwear underneath to fight the heat.

They got to work. Another crew ahead of them had already inserted the plastic liner, so Rod and Leonard and two helpers stabbed the two ends of the steel pipe together and put the bolts through the flanges finger-tight. Colin and Barney would come up behind them later and tighten the bolts completely with the air guns, which were back in service.

A young Ecuadorean soldier sat on a pipe beside Leonard and Rod and the two locals, watching them work as he had for the past eleven days. His machine gun sat beside him.

As Rod laboured, he faced the jungle. Enormous ferns and thick, drooping leaves hung mere metres from his face. Leonard faced the road. Less than 100 meters away sat a shack with a tin roof. Oil trucks, taxis and passenger buses rumbled past, kicking up dust. Monkeys flashed and fluttered through the tops of the trees, chattering the morning away. *A Routine Assignment*

It was 11 a.m. when Rod straightened to wipe the sweat from his face and the fifteen intruders appeared out of nowhere, attacking the young soldier sitting on the pipeline and marching Rod and Leonard into the jungle.

Their job was over.

Fear and Disbelief

"IT'S SOMETHING BIGGER," Sabine Roblain repeated to Rod as they knelt on the vine-strewn jungle floor, their attackers' M-16s levelled at their heads.

But he knew she would say no more, no matter how much he fished for information; she was too frightened. Rod's co-workers—Barney, Colin and Leonard—were silent, as well. He was left with his own thoughts spiralling darkly out of control. *If it's not a fucking robbery, what is it? Murder? If it's murder, when are they going to pull the trigger?*

Before he could come up with an answer, the four United workers, Sabine, Ander, Jesus, Maria, Sonia and the ecotourists' driver were ordered to pick up the kidnappers' backpacks and march back to the road. There were more packs than people, so Rod was forced to carry an extra pack. It was a struggle; his legs and knees were so shaky, he could barely manage one.

When they reached the gravel road, the abductors, without explanation, announced that Sonia and the tourists' driver—the only two Ecuadoreans in the group—could go. "Sorry to have bothered you," one said to Sonia, who now had to leave the scene, and her terrified friends Sabine and Ander, behind.

The hostages, now numbering eight, were marched up the ditch beside the road. Dozens of travellers ordered from their vehicles as well as curious farmers and locals who'd flocked to the scene watched them pass from a safe distance. Some of them lowered their eyes or averted their gaze when he looked at them. Rod knew they weren't about to get involved.

The attackers had two trucks with huge, open-air boxes waiting on the road. Sabine, Ander, Jesus and Maria were herded into the back of one. Just as Rod, Leonard, Colin and Barney were being pushed into another, Barry Meyer rolled up in a company pick-up with his army escort.

The kidnappers jammed their guns through the truck's window, disarming the Ecuadorean soldier without much effort. Barry, stunned by this turn of events, was ordered into the truck that held Rod and the others.

These guys sure seem to know who they're looking for, Rod thought.

The two trucks sped along the gravel road toward the other groups of United workers spread down the line. Dust fanned out behind them and hung in the oppressive air. The backpacks jumped about in the truck's box like popcorn, but every time Rod tried to steady them, a kidnapper smacked his hand with a gun barrel. Rod would soon learn the packs were jammed with plastic explosives.

The vehicles passed United's first fusion tent, a white canvas tarp pulled over a three-metre-tall steel frame erected to keep the plastic liners safe from the heat, dust and rain. A few of the local Ecuadoreans hired by United were there, and the two men who'd warned Rod just days before that something bad was coming down shook their heads as the sinister convoy roared by.

A few hundred metres down the road, the trucks rounded a curve and bore down on the second fusion site. Suddenly, both vehicles slammed on their brakes, skidding in the gravel, and a dozen attackers leapt from the boxes and sprayed the jungle with machine-gun fire. The pipeliners and tourists cowered in the trucks' boxes. The air was instantly blue and saturated with the thick, acrid stench of gunpowder. Rod flinched as hot, spent shells popped from the weapons and struck him in the face.

Rod wondered what they were firing at—until he saw Edison Jacome, a twenty-two-year-old Ecuadorean soldier who had guarded the United workers since the beginning of the job. The guerrillas cut Edison down before he could squeeze off a single shot in return. The young soldier was hit five times, in the torso, in the legs, in the head; Rod saw Edison's body twitch with the impacts like a tangled marionette. He crumpled and fell to the ground, as bullets shredded the foliage and scarred the pipeline behind him. Edison lifted one of his arms, perhaps to motion for help, before it flopped at a grotesque angle behind his back.

Reeling from the shock of seeing Edison killed, Rod looked over at the fusion tent, ripped to ribbons by gunfire. Jesus Christ! Rod thought, Neil's in that tent!

Rod watched as the guerrillas who had killed Edison walked to the tent, pulled open its canvas entrance and found Neil, lying on his stomach, his hands over his ears, alive. Miraculously, he'd not even been hit. At the first sound of gunfire, Neil hit the deck. His instincts saved his life.

As the murderers pushed Neil into the truck with the pipeliners, the other guerrillas circled the fusion site, searching for more Canadians. They immediately spotted one: Steven Brent, the pipeliner everybody called Skunk. At the sound of gunfire, Skunk took off running beside the pipeline away from the fusion tent. The guerrillas fired at Skunk and nearly hit him; the bullets pinged off the pipeline, scarring it. Skunk dove beside the pipe to hide, but the guerrillas grabbed him by the neck of his coveralls and dragged him back to the truck. The pipeliners in the vehicle's box screamed "Canadian! Canadian!" at the guerrillas, worried the attackers were about to execute Skunk for running and hoping they would show mercy because he wasn't American. The camouflaged aggressors did not shoot again, but pushed Skunk into the truck, his hands laced behind his head, his face ashen and streaked with tears.

"I've had enough," Skunk said. "I want to go home."

Barry Meyer, the pipeliners' boss, shook his head and said: "I wish I could send all you guys home."

Grant Rankin, the remaining Canadian, was captured seconds later. When Edison was shot, Grant had been a few hundred metres up the road, pulling pipeline sections into place with the help of an Ecuadorean front-end loader driver. The sound of disturbance was faint, and Grant assumed that it was a work-related problem, that the other men might need the front-end loader to clear the road. So Grant and the loader operator drove straight into the guerrilla mob where he was quickly captured and thrown into the truck with the other pipeliners.

That made twelve hostages—the eight United workers, Sabine Roblain and Spaniards Ander, Jesus and Maria. Without a pause or word of explanation, the fifteen guerrillas ordered their dozen captives out of the trucks and toward the bush.

The guerrillas appeared to be accustomed to traversing the jungle and were nimble and deft on their feet. Rod watched the lone female guerrilla pull her earrings from her ears and toss them into the bush without breaking stride.

But the oil workers and the Spanish tourists, unused to the overgrown terrain, had difficulty keeping up. Slippery vines tangled around their feet and razor-sharp plants slashed their bodies as they ploughed through. The noontime sun pounded down through the layers of foliage onto the backs of their necks. To make matters worse, the oil workers were weighed down by the guerrillas' packs. Rod was again forced to carry two packs, one on his back and one strapped around his chest.

That was just the physical grind. Emotionally, they were all wrecks, in various states of disbelief, panic and shock. Each of the fifteen guerrillas was armed to the teeth, with machine guns, automatic pistols, machetes, daggers. They'd killed Edison Jacome with sudden violence. If the hostages did not co-operate with their captors' wishes, surely they would be killed, too.

That knowledge weighed on Rod with every heavy step. He was near the head of the single-file line of guerrillas and hostages, separated from the rest of his United compadres by at least two kidnappers with machine guns. It appeared to Rod that the kidnappers arranged the line this way—a hostage, then a couple of men with guns—so that ample backup was always nearby in case a hostage tried to escape or overpower one of the guerrillas.

Obviously, there was no chance of physically overwhelming all fifteen guerrillas, but running seemed so, so tempting. A few minutes into the march, he contemplated dropping his backpacks and sprinting through the jungle. But no sooner did he raise his eyes from the path to scan the trees for possible escape routes, than the guerrillas, seeming to sense what he was thinking, moved in closer around him.

After several minutes tramping through the jungle, the guerrillas stopped the group, sat the hostages down on the jungle floor and offered them each a drink of water from their water bottles. Four or five of the kidnappers moved away from the group to talk. Judging by their gestures and agitated body language, Rod guessed that something had gone wrong in the capture, that the original plan had not involved walking through the jungle right away.

The break gave Rod a chance to catch his breath and steal his first good look at his attackers. The guerrillas wore handkerchiefs around their necks with war sayings in English such as "Kill Them All, Let God Sort Them Out." They ranged in age from eighteen to late fifties. Several black-haired young men in their late teens and early twenties appeared to be in spectacular shape. The oldest guerrilla, who led the march and appeared to be the group's scout, was a wizened, hunched man with narrow, darting eyes and grey hair. The lone woman, black-haired and brown-eyed, was in her late teens or early twenties, and her fine, delicate features were obvious even through her face paint. The man who seemed to be the guerrillas' commander was in his forties, with a strong, stocky build and a well-trimmed beard and moustache, like a young Fidel Castro, Rod thought. The commander wore a handkerchief showing a skull with a red bandana and a dagger through it. Rod experienced a sickening sense of déjà vu; he was sure he'd seen the commander and the young woman earlier in the month driving a truck down the gravel highway near Tarapoa. He also thought he'd seen two of the other guerrillas during an equipment run to Lago Agrio.

They've been watching us for days, Rod thought. They knew who they wanted, and they waited until the time was right to get us.

The break was over. Rod and the others moved to strap on the heavy backpacks, but the guerrillas shook their heads. "*Vamoose*," they said. The kidnappers would carry the packs themselves. It was clear they wanted to make better time.

As the hostages marched deeper into the jungle, Rod lost track of the direction. He had a vague impression they were travelling northeast, maybe northwest, but he couldn't be sure.

Though he was concentrating on keeping up, Rod was aware enough of the surroundings to grow amazed at the variety of plants in the rainforest. The sheer enormity of some of the trees was beyond belief. The group walked by ceiba trees that grew straight up for fifty metres before the first branches began, and palm trees supported by odd, huge roots that looked like stilts. Hundreds of colourful exotic plants spread out over the jungle floor. The foliage gave off a warm reek of decomposition, like an enormous compost heap.

Rod was also amazed by the insects. He saw butterflies with wings in various vibrant colours and a kind of caterpillar, with teeth and a sharp hook on its tail, in beautiful shades of fluorescent purple and yellow. A different caterpillar managed to make itself look like the head of a viper. Another camouflaged itself to look like bird droppings.

Rod kept his eyes out for Congo ants—black, stinging insects the size of a double-A battery. Back on the pipeline, the Ecuadoreans warned that three bites from the Congo could kill him.

Two hours into the walk, the hostages came face-to-face with another potentially deadly creature: an enormous snake—an anaconda, perhaps—sunning itself on a fallen log. The guerrillas spied it first and stopped dead in their tracks. One kidnapper slowly withdrew his machete from his sheath, the metal blade making a hissing sound against the leather. Suddenly the snake darted from the log and shot down the trail, sending guerrillas and hostages alike spilling to the trail's sides. The guerrillas chopped at it now with their machetes, swinging the weapons in high, lightning-fast arcs, but they were too slow.

Not long after, Rod heard screams from the line behind him. Barney, labouring heavily and still not fully recovered from his bout of heat stroke on the pipeline two days before, was being attacked by bees. They flew inside his coveralls and stung him repeatedly—da-da-da-da-da, like machine-gun fire. Barney screamed, whipped off his coveralls and swatted at the bees. Each appeared to be about five centimetres long. Rod watched a guerrilla raise a finger to his lips and mime a throat-slitting motion with his hand, the signal for the punishment Barney could expect if he made any noise.

"*Ejército,*" the guerrilla said. Army. There was army all round. The guerrilla made a quiet whirring sound and moved his index finger in a circle. Helicopters.

If the soldiers spot us, the guerrillas will rip the jungle apart with gunfire and use us as body shields. If the army finds us, we're dead. If the snakes or the ants get us, we're dead. If we catch malaria or cholera, we're dead.

Rod thought about Barney's bee attack and worried about his friend's asthma inhaler. It would soon be empty and Barney needed it, especially if he had to endure marches in extreme heat.

More despairing than he had ever felt in his life, Rod had no choice but to keep trudging ahead.

The hostages hiked for more than six hours that first day. During all this time they ate nothing, stopping only rarely for sips of water. At dusk, the forced march finally came to an end in a less dense area of the jungle. The hostages were instructed to sit in a circle. The guerrillas passed along a message to Sabine and Ander: the captors would feed their hostages now.

In muted whispers, the pipeliners asked one another how they were doing. Replies were monosyllabic, barely audible.

No one felt much like talking. Or eating, for that matter, once they saw what the kidnappers had prepared for their first meal—rice, burned to a charcoal black on an open flame. The hostages were given no spoons so they fished chunks of the rice out of the pot with their bare hands, then passed it on.

After their meal of burnt rice, the guerrillas gave each of the men cigarettes, the only saving grace in what had been the worst day of their lives. All the United workers were long-time smokers, except Leonard Carter, but even Leonard sparked one up.

The guerrillas made the hostages a makeshift shelter by stretching a tarp between two trees, creating a narrow, shallow crawl space barely a metre high, then laid wide leaves on the ground to cover the thousands of crawling ants and other insects, their only consideration to the hostages' comfort.

By now, the heat had receded and it became surprisingly chilly, nearly see-your-breath cold. The dozen hostages huddled together under the tarp. How long would they be held by these dangerous, violent, unpredictable men? Would they ever see home again?

REPErCUSSiONS

IT WAS A LAZY WEEKEND morning like any other at the Dunbar house in Edmonton's west end. The bright, early September sun leaked in through the curtained windows as Jane Dunbar and her seven-year-old daughter Krissy sat playing in the basement, cartoons noisy in the background. The phone rang upstairs, but Jane did not hear it over the blare of the TV.

"Mom, it's the phone," said Krissy, a round-faced redhead who had her mother's fiery temper. "Get the phone!"

Jane darted up the stairs and grabbed the phone just after it rang for the third and final time. She waited for the caller to leave a message on the voice mail, but no one did. Luckily, the call display revealed where the call was from. "United Pipeline Systems," it said, also listing the telephone number at her husband's company's east Edmonton office.

It was September 11, a Saturday. *Why would United be calling me today? Maybe Rod decided to come home early from the job in Ecuador after all. Maybe he decided enough is enough.*

But she realized that couldn't be the case. *He wouldn't jump on a plane without telling me. He's dead. Rod's dead.*

She grabbed the phone and dialed United's number. No answer. She tried again. No answer. Tried again. No answer.

Her mind flashed back to the conversation she'd had with Rod two nights ago on The Block's satellite phone. She remembered how tense and guarded he'd sounded, as if he were hiding something important from her.

Jane tried to remain calm as she made her daughter lunch. While Krissy ate, Jane sat at the kitchen table, lit a cigarette and waited to hear whether her husband was dead or alive.

She tried to do crossword puzzles but couldn't concentrate. She couldn't stop thinking of her life with Rod. It seemed like a lifetime though they'd been married only nine years.

They first met in a Grade 7 class in a west-end Edmonton junior high school, but there was no grade-school romance, no puppy love between them. After junior high their paths diverged and didn't cross again until the late 1980s, when Jane ran into Rod at a local pub. He wore a leather jacket, rode a Harley and sported several tattoos. He had a good, steady job with a local pipeline company.

Rod was the best of both worlds: part Harley-riding bad boy, part responsible grown-up. Sparks flew. Jane was hooked and the couple was married in 1990.

Two years later Krissy was born. Rod nicknamed her Tweet because she was so quiet at first, her cries sounded like tiny bird calls. But Krissy discovered her vocal cords at three months and controlled the house from then on.

Now, here was Krissy, just minutes after United had called, wanting to tie up the phone. "Mom, can I call a friend?" Krissy asked.

Jane told Krissy she was sorry, but there would be no phone calls allowed. Jane didn't want to miss another call from United.

While Krissy retreated to her room to watch cartoons for most of the afternoon, Jane ran through in her head some possible options for United's call—Rod was injured on the job; he was beat up and robbed by destitute locals. She didn't want to believe any of them and dismissed them all, growing more impatient by the minute.

At 5, the phone finally rang again. It was Ken Foster, Rod's boss and United Pipeline's general manager, calling from the Edmonton office.

"Have you heard yet?" Foster asked.

"Have I heard what?"

Foster matter-of-factly explained that Rod and seven of his co-workers had been nabbed by armed guerrillas on the job site in Ecuador. No one knew the identity of the guerrillas or why they had kidnapped the pipeliners.

It was as if a little switch clicked in Jane's head, and she lashed out. "You son of a bitch!" Jane screamed. "Why the hell did you send him down there?" She shrieked and swore, calling Foster every dirty name she knew, and started to sob.

"What do you think it is?" Jane said, through tears. "Money, political, what? Is it about money?"

Foster was non-committal. They didn't know why the men had been kidnapped. They didn't know who was responsible. And they didn't know for sure when or if they'd ever be seen or heard from again.

"How do you even know this?" Jane asked.

"One of the guys escaped," Foster said.

Max Shaw, the Australian-born United worker from Calgary, Foster explained, was working on the pipeline but managed to hide in the jungle and escaped undetected when the violence broke out. Max ran away from the guerrillas, commandeered a vehicle and drove it back to The Block. There, he phoned his Calgary roommate to pass along his family's phone numbers in case the compound was overtaken. Then he called Rob Mackie, United's manager back in Edmonton, to break the bad news about the capture.

Kirk Theige, the project's other supervisor, was away from the job site on a parts run to Lago Agrio and missed the whole kidnapping.

Just our luck, Jane thought. Of course Rod wouldn't be the one to escape.

Krissy came out of her room, frightened by her mother's screams. At first, Jane was too busy yelling at Rod's boss to notice her daughter.

"What's the matter with Daddy?" Krissy said, standing by the sink, tears already streaming down her cheeks. "What's the matter with Daddy?"

Jane looked at Krissy and stopped. "I have to go," Jane told Foster.

"Don't be telling people who don't need to know," Foster said before Jane could hang up.

She balked. "Well, I'm telling his mom, my mom, his sisters . . ."

"Yes, you can tell family, just don't tell anybody who isn't family," he said. "We're trying to keep it out of the media as long as we can, but it won't be long before they find out."

Foster asked her to come to a meeting for family members of the kidnapped men the next day—Sunday—at 10 a.m. Jane slammed down the phone without saying good-bye and rushed to her daughter's side.

"He's OK," she said, and stopped crying. "It's just some men—there are bad people down there. They're going to let Daddy go."

Jane hugged her daughter and, almost in a trance, she called every relative she could think of, worried they'd find out what had happened in the newspaper or on TV. She was in shock, but the more she told the story, the more it sunk in.

Everyone wanted to come over to her house to comfort her—her mother, Rod's mother, Rod's sisters, her brother. The phone rang constantly as the news travelled. The offers of help were well-intentioned, but Jane grew frustrated and impatient with them.

By 8 p.m., Jane was exhausted but still flushed with terror. She was relieved when Krissy asked if she could sleep in Rod and Jane's bed. Jane quickly said yes—she didn't want to sleep by herself, either.

Krissy brushed her teeth, washed her face and climbed into bed, wearing a pair of Rod's boxer shorts and a T-shirt. A tomboy, Krissy hated nightgowns. Instead, she raided the pile of boxer shorts Rod had never worn—the ones covered in hearts and cartoon characters Jane bought him for Christmas and Valentine's.

Jane tucked her daughter under the covers. She was crying again.

"Do you promise Daddy's going to come home?" Krissy asked.

"I promise, Krissy. I promise."

Jane double-checked the deadbolts on the front and back doors. She punched her code into the lighted keypad to set the alarm system. She let their German shepherd, Sheba, into the house, then entered the bedroom and locked the door. She kept the panic button that came with the alarm system by her side.

Jane wasn't normally one to even think about a panic button. She usually went to sleep without even locking the door. But tonight was different. She'd lost faith in the world today. If men with guns could kidnap Rod, men with guns could break into her house, too.

Jane crawled into bed and tried to sleep. She noticed every creak of the pipes, every sound.

She felt guilty, lying in a comfortable bed under warm blankets. *Where is Rod sleeping? Is he sleeping at all?*

The abduction of the United Pipeline workers sparked a frenzy of activity and emotion across North America in the hours after the guerrillas and their captives disappeared into the Ecuadorean jungle. Ken Foster, an engineer and oilfield boss who'd moved from England to Edmonton twenty years earlier, spent the afternoon calling mothers, fathers and wives to tell them of the kidnapping. Some, like Jane Dunbar, exploded in anger. They yelled, swore and blamed him. Others sobbed quietly. Still others refused to believe him.

Foster scheduled a conference call with Foreign Affairs officials in Ottawa and Ecuador for 8 a.m. Sunday morning. The families of the hostages were to be debriefed at a 10 a.m. meeting.

He also contacted a media specialist from Calgary to help deal with the expected onslaught of media interest, and two American firms to begin working on the arduous task of freeing the men from their jungle prison. One, the Miami-based Ackerman Group, which included former members of the U.S.'s Central Intelligence Agency, would directly negotiate with the guerrillas for the hostages' release, if and when the kidnappers chose to make contact. The second, a Missouri firm called Allied Intelligence, was charged with setting up safe houses in Ecuador for the negotiators and with making preparations for the pipeliners' safe transfer back to North America. United had to hire private firms because the Canadian government—with its infinitely deep pockets—refuses to negotiate with kidnappers. The feds' policy is that it's up to the company involved to come to an agreement with the kidnappers and to pay a negotiated ransom, if one is demanded.

After a sleepless night, Foster and Mackie arrived at United's Edmonton office Sunday morning for the 8 a.m. call. On the line were Helen Harris, director of emergency services for Foreign Affairs, and Gar Pardy, Canada's director general of consular affairs. They were joined by members of an emergency task force in South America and Canada.

Foreign Affairs officials heard the news of the Ecuador kidnapping Saturday afternoon while on the phone discussing the violent election-related uprisings in East Timor with American State Department officials in Washington. When the word broke, several things happened simultaneously. The clock in the operations centre of Foreign Affairs in Ottawa was set to Quito time. Extra staff were brought in to answer phone calls from anguished family members and news reporters. Officials plotted strategy with John Kneale, Canada's ambassador to Ecuador, and Kneale immediately began seeking information from ALER and City Investing representatives in Quito.

Foreign Affairs told Foster the Ecuadorean government had made promises at the highest diplomatic levels that everything that could be done would be done. The army had dispatched troops, along with a special anti-kidnapping unit of the Ecuadorean police, to comb the dense jungle for the hostages. Police had sealed off the area and the military had set up checkpoints along the major roads surrounding the kidnapping site. Soldiers with machine guns had checked thousands of vehicles in Sucumbios province hoping to identify anyone supplying the guerrillas with food, clothing and other necessities.

But no one was able to say what would happen if the army did find the guerrillas in the jungle. Foreign Affairs was worried that a confrontation could easily precipitate violence and the deaths of some or all of the hostages. The guerrillas had already killed one soldier and there was no telling what they would do if confronted by the military.

Foreign Affairs worried that one of the pipeliners, or Sabine or one of the Spanish ecotourists, would try—and fail—to escape. Though Canadian diplomats had no idea who the kidnappers were, they knew any guerrilla group would surely kill a hostage who tried to flee.

Foreign Affairs also worried that the guerrillas might decide they'd bitten off more than they could chew, and would murder the hostages before disappearing into the Latin American underground to escape the wrath of international authorities.

They were also concerned that the Canadian families of the hostages might reveal intimate details about their loved ones to the media, and that these details might be discovered by the guerrillas on the Internet and then exploited. Fatal consequences might result if the guerrillas discovered that one of the hostages was of a disagreeable religious faith. If the guerrillas, for example, were Roman Catholic, Ecuador's predominant religion, perhaps they would treat a Jewish captive harshly. Or negotiations might be severely affected if it were revealed that one of the pipeliners was independently wealthy. Pardy gave Foster a pressing example to illustrate his concern: Spanish officials were already apprehensive that the guerrillas might discover that Jesus Magunagoicoechea was a police officer in Bilbao, Spain.

Foreign Affairs was also concerned because the kidnapping had occurred in Ecuador, where there are relatively few abductions. Canadian diplomats had previous experience dealing with kidnappings in Colombia, where some 2,000 occur each year. In Ecuador there would be different diplomatic protocols and different potentially responsible groups to consider.

Pardy and Harris told Foster he must be straight with the families on one point: the negotiations for the hostages' release would be a long, drawn-out affair. In one case in Colombia, authorities didn't hear from the kidnappers for ten months. Foreign Affairs urged that the Edmonton families organize their lives around that reality.

After an hour, the meeting with Foreign Affairs wrapped up. It was time for United to meet the families.

———

Jane didn't know what to expect from the meeting, held in the boardroom of a Holiday Inn a few blocks from United's office, in an east Edmonton industrial park. She wished somebody would take the microphone and announce this was all a cruel joke.

Jane had been either crying or near tears since hearing the news Saturday afternoon from Ken Foster. Now she walked with her parents into the conference room. The first person she spotted was Barry's wife, Esther, her old neighbour from the acreage near Devon, just southwest of Edmonton. Tears streaming down her cheeks, Esther rushed towards Jane and the two women collapsed in each other's arms.

"This can't be happening," Jane said in a muffled voice. "This can't be happening. It just sounds so fictitious. I know they were taken, but do you know anything more?" Esther shook her head no.

Colin Fraser's wife Karen rushed over and hugged Jane. Jane knew Karen from company golf tournaments. Rod, Jane, Karen and Colin often went out for drinks afterwards and chatted like old friends. Karen's youngest child was the same age as Krissy and she and Jane would swap stories about the kids.

Everywhere Jane looked there was a familiar face streaked with tears and contorted in pain. After speaking with Karen, Jane spotted Sean Watt, Brant Scheelar's older brother and a former United worker.

Oh my God, they've got Barney, too.

She hated the thought of Barney being captured, but it comforted her to know Rod was among friends. Jane knew Barney, Rod, Colin and Barry would keep their spirits up and look after one another. She prayed they wouldn't be split up. If one of them gets sick, the guerrillas won't care, she thought. Rod will only have the others to lean on.

The meeting was called to order. Family members filed into rows of chairs set up at the front of the room. Foster repeated to the families what he knew, which wasn't much. It was the same story—the men had been taken by about fifteen gun-toting guerrillas, outfitted in camouflage gear and painted faces. They had been rushed into the thick, snake-infested jungle, along with four tourists—three Spaniards and a Canadian.

No one knew who was responsible, but the motive was most likely money. No Canadians had ever been kidnapped in Ecuador before, the United officials said, but kidnapping was a booming business in neighbouring Colombia, whose southern border is only about forty kilometres away from the City Investing–owned pipeline the men were repairing. It might take a month or even longer to even hear from the kidnappers, Foster said.

Foster passed along to the family members a twenty-four-hour phone number staffed by Foreign Affairs officials where they could call for free counselling, but Jane wasn't interested. She didn't feel like talking to anybody—much less a stranger. How could they understand? If the counsellors could bring Rod home, fine. If they couldn't, what was the use in talking to them?

Foster told the families not to talk to reporters under any circumstances. Foster's Calgary media consultant stressed to the families the importance of staying quiet, no matter how much they were harassed. The kidnappers might be a highly organized group with access to the Internet. They could be monitoring Edmonton and national newspapers to see if the families had said anything. Any kind of public pressure or outcry from the families might cause a ransom demand to soar and the hostages' time in captivity to increase as well. Any kind of comment could cost the hostages their lives.

Though Jane was bursting with questions, she said very little at the meeting. She sat and cried and let her father, a former soldier with the Canadian military, do the talking. He wanted to know if the Ecuadorean army was going into the jungle with guns blazing. He knew a confrontation could mean Rod's death. Foster told him the Canadian diplomats had the same concerns, and would stress them to the proper Ecuadorean authorities.

It wasn't until Jane had left the meeting that the reality sunk in. *This isn't just a bad dream. It's real. Rod may never come home. He may die in that jungle.*

Later that day, Ecuadorean police released the names of the eight kidnapped oil workers to the international media, but they weren't close to getting the spelling right. Barry Meyer was listed as Harry Mayer, Brant Scheelar was listed as Brad Scheler. But most strange was Rod. The police's press release said his name was Raft Pumbar.

"Rod's finally famous, and they haven't even got his name right," said Rod's sister, Twyla.

But as the day wore on and the media dug deeper into the story, the reporters started to get the story straight and were able to nail down the correct names of the men taken. Of all the hostages, Rod's family was the easiest to find. They were in the phone book: Dunbar, Rod & J.

It wasn't in Jane's nature to hang up on people who called. She couldn't resist the temptation to say at least something to reporters.

When the first media call came that Sunday, Jane confirmed they had the right house and that she was Rod's wife. Before hanging up, she said, "We're doing fine," the only comment by a family member of the hostages that made Monday morning's newspapers.

In fact Jane was doing anything but fine. In a blur, she contacted a neighbour who worked at Krissy's elementary school and told her she was worried that reporters might accost Krissy on the school grounds.

"Can you do me a favour?" Jane asked. "Can you please just keep an eye on her and make sure no one approaches her?"

After another restless night, Jane drove Krissy to school. She knew she looked awful, with dark bags under eyes. Her long, blond hair was frizzy and tangled. But Krissy needed some normalcy in her life; she needed her mother to drive her to school just as before.

At school, Jane met with the principal, told him what had happened and asked the teachers to be understanding if her daughter suddenly started crying or acting up.

Then Jane drove the few blocks home, sat down at the kitchen table and lit a cigarette.

The wait had begun.

Questions of Identity

THE HOSTAGES' FIRST night in the jungle was not a pleasant one. Some of them managed to sleep, but fitfully, with cluttered, anxious dreams. Others spent the night in an almost hyper-caffeinated state, their adrenaline and fear more potent than the strongest coffee. Rod, an irregular sleeper at the best of times, lay board-stiff, crammed together with his fellow captives under their makeshift tent, listening to the rainforest's odd sounds. The mournful cries of howler monkeys echoed the wind shrieking through the trees. Macaws, true to their name, cawed throughout the night. But the most sinister noises were the crunching foot-steps of the guerrillas as they paced the jungle floor in front of the hostages' tent, whispering in staccato bursts of Spanish. Without those sounds, Rod might have fooled himself into thinking this was all a horrible, vivid dream.

Just before daybreak, Rod and the others were roused from their uneasy slumber and forced to march again through the thick foliage. The early wake-up call was to become a staple of the guerrillas' punishing regimen.

The humidity rose with the sun. Soon wet patches of sweat bloomed through his coveralls. Although he was in tremendous shape—six feet tall, about 200 pounds, very little body fat—he wasn't used to setting such a quick pace over awkward terrain. His breathing laboured within minutes. His face was battered by the rainforest's heavy leaves and thick branches. He wanted nothing more than to sit, cross-legged, in the middle of the trail and rest.

But there was a machine gun in his back, so he kept on.

After hours of trudging, the guerrillas finally stopped and passed canteens of water around. While Jane Dunbar and the other hostages' families gathered to meet in the Edmonton hotel conference room, Rod and his fellow captives were positioned in a circle and told to keep quiet. "*Ejército*," one guerrilla said. Again, the kidnappers feared the army was all around.

The kidnappers' moustachioed commander and his lieutenants huddled in a tight group about five metres from the United workers. They whispered together for a few minutes. Finally, the commander approached the pipeliners and, with hand gestures and rudimentary Spanish the Canadians could understand, asked about the workers' chain of command.

Rod didn't know what the pipeliners' hierarchy had to do with anything, and didn't answer, but Colin piped up. He pointed to Barry, the supervisor, then Rod, the crew's *de facto* foreman, then Leonard, then himself. It wasn't clear why the commander wanted to know, but Colin's answer seemed to satisfy him.

Then Neil stood up and, in deliberate English, he looked straight at the commander and said: "What's this all about? Are you going to kill us?" The commander didn't appear to understand him, so Neil dragged a finger slowly across his neck in a throat-slitting motion.

The commander understood that. "No, no," he said, rubbing his index and middle fingers together against his thumb. "Money."

Neil reached into the pocket of his coveralls. Inside was about 5,000 sucres, Ecuadorean currency worth about 50 cents Canadian. "Here," he said, and offered it to the commander. Rod watched the head guerrilla smile and shake his head. It was not nearly enough.

Sabine was right. It's something bigger. They want big money. And they're not going to let us go home until they get it.

————

The guerrillas' motives were not so immediately clear to the outside world. Theories about the kidnappers' identities swirled like dust kicked up on the Lago Agrio–Tarapoa gravel highway. The capture was huge news in Canada and even bigger news in Ecuador, where the size of the attack stunned the military, the government and the public. Sucumbios province had seen kidnappings before—local businessmen, mostly, taken by cash-hungry bandits—but it had never experienced a mass kidnapping of foreigners and tourists.

Coverage in Quito and Edmonton newspapers reached saturation levels, and all of it pointed to two left-wing Colombian guerrilla groups as the most likely suspects—FARC, translated into English as the Revolutionary Armed Forces of Colombia, a 15,000-strong Marxist rebel army engaged in a thirty-five-year civil war with the Colombian government, and ELN, known in English as the National Liberation Army, an equally violent 5,000-member group said to be responsible, along with FARC, for 70 per cent of Colombia's 2,000 yearly kidnappings.

The ELN was considered a prime suspect for two main reasons: its penchant for kidnapping, and its virulent anti-petroleum stance. In October 1998, ELN rebels had blasted Colombia's largest oil pipeline, killing more than fifty people, and observers reasoned they may have kidnapped the Canadian oil workers to make a political point.

But the pro-Cuban ELN had no recorded presence in Colombia's Putomayo province, which borders Ecuador north of Lago Agrio. The area was an undisguised FARC stronghold. In fact, the bigger rebel group ran a sort of mini-Marxist state there, in a 42,000 sq.-km demilitarized zone (DMZ) handed to it by the Colombian government as a peacekeeping gesture. FARC financed its insurrection against the Colombian government by protecting cocaine farmers and with ransom money from its kidnappings. Rumours had it that FARC held hundreds of hostages in camps in the DMZ. It was said they had pockets of local support in other parts of Colombia, where they could hold their hostages. They employed community sympathizers who monitored the countryside for anti-guerrilla activity.

FARC was well organized, with its own Internet website and representatives all over the world, including Canada. It rationalized its kidnappings to gain public sympathy. FARC said the Colombian government financed its war effort against left-wing rebels by levying industry taxes on the nation's rich. FARC replied to the government with what it called "detentions"—kidnappings aimed at extracting a parallel war tax from Colombia's wealthy. It used the money to purchase state-of-the-art weapons to fight Colombia's government, and had several ultimate goals: nationalization of Colombia's resources, independent local control of some rural areas, an end to what it called the country's political death squads and the unification of the countries of Colombia, Ecuador and Venezuela.

In years prior to the kidnapping of the United workers, FARC had become infamous in the Putomayo region of Colombia for a tactic called *la pesca milagrosa*, or miraculous fishing expedition, named after a biblical story in which Jesus calls upon his disciples to become "fishers of men." The tactic, which involved setting up roadblocks and kidnapping anybody who appeared to be ransom-worthy, had netted FARC dozens of hostages.

Although they claimed to respect Ecuador's border, FARC rebels were notorious for crossing into the Oriente. Ecuadorean peasants in the area had taken to calling FARC rebels *"hombres de la montana"* or "men of the mountain" after seeing the camouflaged guerrillas cross the border. Furthermore, Lago Agrio was rumoured to be a favoured vacation haunt for FARC members on furlough. In 1997, 100 FARC guerrillas had a shootout with Ecuadorean police near the Colombian border north of Tarapoa. Four officers died.

All that history made FARC a likely candidate. But there were other, subtler factors involved in the finger-pointing. FARC had a previous, well-known Canadian connection: it held Albertan diamond miner Norbert Reinhart hostage for ninety-four days in the Colombian hills. Reinhart was released in January 1999 after his company paid FARC more than $100,000 in ransom. Reinhart's ordeal became famous after he traded places with co-worker and fellow Canadian Ed Leonard, who had spent 106 days with FARC in captivity after he was abducted from a Greystar Resources Ltd. mine in northeastern Colombia. Less than five months after Reinhart's dramatic release and triumphant return to Canada, he separated from his Canadian wife and returned to Colombia, reportedly to visit his Colombian girlfriend and to resume his commercial interests there. Some in the area believed Reinhart had links with FARC sympathizers prior to the kidnapping and that his decision to swap places with Leonard only complicated the situation. Whatever the case, Latin American experts cited the Reinhart/Leonard incident as evidence that FARC was now fishing for foreigners, and that the United workers were likely its latest catch.

Eyewitness accounts of the United Pipeline kidnapping fuelled the speculation. In interviews after the abduction with Ecuadorean authorities and the press, Sonia Falcon, the Quito radio worker let free by the kidnappers because she was Ecuadorean, reported that the attackers appeared to be Colombian.

"They didn't identify themselves by the name of any group, but I knew they were Colombians from their accent," she said. Falcon also said the kidnappers used radios, disguised their identities with facepaint, moved with military precision and called their commander "Commandant," all reputed to be hallmarks of the FARC.

Another eyewitness was off-duty police officer Angel Manzano, who was working as a security guard for another oil company when he happened upon the abduction as it unfolded. Manzano, who'd approached the kidnappers' roadblock in his truck, was stripped of his gun and ammunition by the guerrillas. He, too, told authorities the captors had Colombian accents.

Canadian newspapers reported these details and others. One paper obtained a preliminary police report of the kidnapping that suggested "suspected Colombian guerrillas" were responsible, and quoted anonymous Ecuadorean authorities who said the hostages were likely in the hands of Frente 48, a FARC special unit that operated in Colombia's Putomayo province. The sources believed the guerrillas, their hostages in tow, had already crossed the massive San Miguel River that borders Ecuador and were back in Colombia, safe from Ecuadorean military reprisals.

Perhaps the most compelling suggestion of FARC involvement came from an anonymous American State Department official, who was quoted as saying the rebels had responded to the Colombian and American governments' requests for peace talks "by kidnapping foreigners," a clear reference to the pipeliners and the Spanish tourists. Behind the scenes, Canadian Foreign Affairs officials marked FARC at the top of their lists of suspects.

All this was apparently too much international heat for FARC's liking. They struck back at the Americans, whose fight to stamp out Colombian drug exports was a cornerstone of their foreign policy, and vehemently denied FARC was involved.

Ivan Rios, one of the rebel group's official spokesmen, said: "They are accusing the FARC of breaking its own word. The FARC has clearly stated that it will not develop activities outside the frontier of our country." In a statement sent by electronic mail to international news organizations and addressed "To World Opinion," FARC said: "We have watched, with patience and indignation, how perverse slander is being used by those interested in promoting the internalization of the Colombian conflict to charge our organization with responsibility for seizing twelve foreigners in the sister Republic of Ecuador. We have repeatedly expressed our position of absolute respect for the territorial sovereignty of the people and government of Ecuador, and of other countries bordering Colombia."

FARC's refutation was accepted by some Latin American experts, who suggested instead that the kidnapping might be the work of right-wing Colombian paramilitaries out to discredit

FARC and further isolate them internationally. Others, however, denied the denial, noting that FARC had lied about its involvement in past crimes and was simply trying to weather another public relations storm. In March 1999, three American environmentalists working with Colombia's indigenous U'wa tribe were kidnapped and found dead by authorities on the Venezuelan border, their bodies hooded and mutilated. They were executed—shot in the head and chest. FARC denied knowledge of the incident until the Colombian army released an intercepted radio message in which a rebel commander clearly ordered the killings. FARC, caught red-handed, admitted responsibility and pledged to punish those involved.

In another case, in July 1999, a Venezuelan airliner with twelve people on board was hijacked. Even though the plane was discovered by FARC guerrillas near the border, the rebels claimed innocence. They reported that the hijackers fled when they arrived. One witness, however, said he saw one of the hijackers dressed in a FARC uniform, saluting one of the commanders.

FARC had lied before; they could be lying again.

Publicly, Ecuadorean military and police said they weren't ruling any group out. The early police report pointing to "suspected Colombian guerrillas" was dismissed as speculation. High-ranking officers said the kidnappers could be FARC, right-wing paramilitaries or common bandits who roamed the highway between Tarapoa and Lago Agrio holding up trucks and buses. For months, local police had been warning tourists to stay away from the area near the Colombian border. Canada's Foreign Affairs department, in a report issued two months before the kidnapping, advised Canadians not to travel to the northern Ecuadorean provinces of Sucumbios and Carchi. "Both areas, as well as elsewhere along the border with Colombia, are dangerous because of the increasing incidence of crime, including extortion and kidnapping," the report said.

Ecuadorean authorities couldn't agree on who was behind the kidnapping, but they did reach consensus on one point: the hostages were in grave danger. Word had reached the military that Barney was asthmatic and might not be able to withstand the rigours of fleeing through the rainforest. Some worried that the hostages might starve if the guerrillas encountered difficulties obtaining supplies.

"[The jungle] is not an easy place to live," said an army captain. "It would be very difficult."

That knowledge, in addition to the pressure the kidnapping placed on Ecuador's tourism industry and foreign profile, prompted a swift military reaction. The army set up a temporary base at The Block in Tarapoa and sent as many as 6,000 soldiers into the jungle between the kidnapping site and the Ecuador/Colombia border.

Among the army patrols was a crack Ecuadorean brigade called the Iwias, which included several Shuar and Achuar Indians. The indigenous groups were expert at jungle survival. They knew which trees would yield water and which snakes could be hacked open with a machete and eaten raw. They were among the fiercest of Ecuadorean soldiers, a sort of spiritually minded Green Beret corps. In centuries past, the Shuar shrank the heads of Spaniards who tried to colonize their land, and continued the practice until as recently as two generations ago.

Despite their dexterity, even the Iwias were only able to proceed slowly through the jungle. The search wasn't helped when frightened locals proved unwilling to share any information they had about the kidnapping. The army tried to grease the wheels with a $3,000 reward—a year's pay for most rural Ecuadoreans—but even that yielded few leads. Twice the military seemed to come close to the guerrillas' path—one soldier found a belt on the search, another an empty bullet box—but so far they'd been unable to find the kidnappers.

Military leaders theorized the guerrillas would probably split the twelve hostages into three smaller groups to make travel easier in the oppressive heat and hostile jungle terrain. But like so much else in the early days following the kidnapping, this was just a wild guess.

———

In fact, on the second day of their ordeal, the twelve hostages were still together, marching in some indeterminate direction away from the army patrols. After Colin had explained United's chain of command to the guerrillas, Barry, the supervisor, was moved to the front of the pack to lead the march, ahead of Rod. But Barry, the oldest hostage and, at six-foot-two, about 250 pounds, one of the biggest, had trouble keeping pace. Several times he collapsed to the ground and the guerrillas ordered Colin and Rod to help him until he recovered. Finally the kidnappers moved Barry to the back of the group, leaving Rod as the lead in the column of captives.

They marched for several hours straight the second day, enduring swarms of insects and intermittent torrents of rain. Always there were crawling and flying bugs to contend with. They nested under roots, in stumps and, most tormenting, lay massed together and hidden on the underside of broad leaves. Keeping his eyes on his feet and the treacherous jungle trail, Rod brushed the leaves with his head and shoulders as he marched, sending hundreds of insects tumbling from the branches, swarming to the back of his neck, stinging and biting.

The guerrillas weren't immune, either. Several times, Rod would hear a yelp from somewhere in the pack and would turn to see a camouflaged figure jumping and flailing wildly at the back of his neck.

The kidnappers, equipped with plastic-bag ponchos, had better luck with the rain. Rod envied the hats they wore, the curved edges shaped to deflect the rain onto the plastic instead of their faces. As they marched, they chopped giant leaves from trees and carried them over their heads. The hostages, who did not have the luxuries of plastic bags, headgear or machetes, suffered through the deluges in their soaked coveralls.

Every couple of hours the guerrillas stopped the march to pass around water, and a soupy mixture of runny oatmeal and plant roots. The hostages gladly took the former, but were too frightened to accept the latter. The concoction might kill them or, at the very least, make them sick. Rod didn't need to eat yet, anyway—he still had adrenaline to go on.

Another break, this time an unscheduled one, provided a surreal moment for the hostages. Suddenly, several of their captors stopped walking and dropped to their hands and knees. One of their cohorts, a clumsy guerrilla the hostages would come to know as Lario, had lost a contact lens. Rod tried desperately not to laugh as the camouflaged men, who twenty-four hours earlier had mercilessly and without hesitation torn apart Edison Jacome, sifted through dirt and leaves on all fours searching for Lario's wayward lens. Lario was looking on the ground with one eye closed, as if he had been poked there by an errant finger. It was pure slapstick, worthy of a Three Stooges movie.

In the end the search proved fruitless, and Lario fetched his glasses from his backpack. He put them on—round, thick lenses with a string attached to the frames—and it was all Rod could do to keep from laughing out loud.

Rod looked at Lario, with his ruler-straight black hair and his magnified eyes, and thought again of a movie, this time an old war flick in which American G.I.s find an old, bespectacled Japanese soldier on a deserted Pacific island thirty years after the fighting had ended. Lario looked exactly like that goggle-eyed soldier, give or take a couple of decades. *This guy's a guerrilla?*

It wasn't long, however, before the kidnappers re-established how deadly serious they were.

All day, helicopters and spotter planes flew overhead, searching for the guerrillas and their hostages. The machines were too close for comfort for the kidnappers. They told Ander and Sabine, the pipeliners' interpreters, the hostages would be killed if they tried to flag down the choppers. The guerrillas said if they were ever discovered, there would be a bloodbath and no one would survive.

The guerrillas were also nervous about the military ground forces, which closed in several times on the hostages. In one particularly tense instance, as the pack approached a low ridge, one of the guerrilla scouts gave a sharp whistle and the remaining kidnappers threw the hostages down to the ground. They retreated to crouched positions several metres behind the pipeliners, and Rod understood they were being used as body shields. If the soldiers did, by some miracle, spot the guerrillas in the trees, they'd have to shoot through the hostages to hit them.

Lying on his stomach, Rod saw one of the guerrillas, a younger man who appeared to be second-in-command, circle around the ridge to investigate. He was gone for several minutes, and Rod started to panic.

How close are these fucking army guys? If they're too close, we're going to find ourselves in the middle of a gunfight.

Suddenly the trees rustled a few metres ahead of the prone hostages, and a guerrilla behind Rod jumped to his feet, training his M-16 on the movement. From behind a palm emerged the guerrillas' second-in-command, returning with news that the coast was clear. He'd almost been shot by his own man.

Later in the day the guerrillas led the hostages down a heavily trampled path to the side of a jungle clearing. Across the clearing, Rod could see swamps and a slight valley where the jungle began again.

The kidnappers paused until the skies were clear of aircraft, then hustled the group across the clearing to the other side. As soon as the hostages made it across the clearing, the guerrillas told them to lie down. They'd seen something in the valley below.

Two of the guerrillas set their backpacks on the ground. To Rod's surprise, both changed from their camouflage suits and put on civilian clothes—Adidas sweatpants and button-down shirts. One of the kidnappers demanded that Sabine hand over her baseball cap, which he put on his head. Then the guerrillas moved out, leaving their backpacks behind but taking their rifles.

Rod didn't know what was happening. Perhaps the valley was some sort of rendezvous point, where they were to meet other guerrillas or a waiting vehicle. But the remaining guerrillas offered no explanation. They crouched and guarded the hostages for two hours, their machine guns cocked and trained constantly on the captives. Rod waited for the sound of gunfire, or voices, or helicopter rotors, but heard nothing. *What the hell is going on?*

Finally, the pair of guerrilla scouts returned to the group. One of them carried an Ecuadorean army issue metal backpack, and a pair of camouflaged army pants. The other held a pair of pants and an Ecuadorean army jacket.

Rod summoned the nerve to ask what had happened. The scout holding the jacket pointed at a military insignia on the garment, said "*Ejército,*" then mimed slitting his throat. The implication was clear—the scouts had managed to surprise two stray army soldiers and had killed them. Whether the guerrillas were lying, or altering their story to put the fear of God into the hostages, was immaterial: after seeing what they'd done to Edison Jacome, Rod had no reason to doubt them.

The scouts threw the pants at Grant, who was short enough to fit into them. One of the scouts kept the metal-frame backpack. Another guerrilla took the remaining pair of pants.

Rod knew Grant would have no compunctions about wearing a dead soldier's uniform. He wished he had the pants himself. They were warm and dry and would keep the bugs at bay.

In this harsh new reality, Rod had no room for guilt, no room for anything except staying alive.

Politics and Cigarettes

LIKE KNIVES WHETTED against a stone, the hostages' tempers grew sharper as their time in captivity stretched from hours into days. Rod tried as hard as he could to stay strong, to maintain a positive attitude, but it was a struggle. In the jungle, he had no release. It was different on the pipeline. There, when he got pissed off, he could scream, swear or smash his aggressions away with a few well-placed blows on the steel with a sledgehammer. Here he was powerless, emasculated by vicious men with guns. Venting at the guerrillas was not an option for him or the other pipeliners. So they turned on each other.

He felt guilty about it, but as the hostages' jungle sentence approached its first week, Rod found himself growing increasingly irritated with his fellow pipeliners and the Spaniards. They got on his nerves, and he was sure the feeling was mutual.

Still, everybody was trying hard to get along. Acts of friendship—reassuring words, pats on the back—helped everybody get through the ordeal. But while he liked Barney, Colin and the rest of the guys, Rod found it a strain spending twenty-four hours a day with them, sharing their body heat under the tarp at night and every begged cigarette during the day.

The food didn't help. It was served only two times a day, at breakfast and supper, and the meals were meagre and awful. Burnt rice, beans, monkey, piranha, the occasional handful of ants or grubs—not exactly staples of the typical North American diet. Breakfast was warmed-up supper from the night before. And meals could take two hours because the hostages were forced to eat out of one bowl, with one spoon.

At supper one night, the guerrillas offered the hostages blistering jalapeno peppers to mix in with their rice and beans. They were too fiery even for Rod, who was used to eating hot food in Texas and Oklahoma, where the locals drench their eggs in Tabasco sauce. Neil didn't want to try the peppers at all, but Rod, ever the prankster, convinced him.

"Come on, Neil, have one," said Rod. "It's mild, it's sweet."

Neil, still suspicious, took a bite from a pepper and immediately spat it out, his mouth on fire and his eyes bulging. He was furious at Rod. The jalapeno gave him canker sores and burnt his lips.

One afternoon a guerrilla tossed a bulging pouch of plain crackers at Rod's feet. The famished Canadian felt as if he'd hit all sevens on a slot machine. He picked up the pouch, and recoiled, wrinkling his nose; it was doused in the fuel the guerrillas used to start their Coleman camp stove. The fuel, a reeking, low-octane, kerosene-type petrol, was so strong it burned Rod's skin. But he and the other pipeliners were so ravenous they ate the crackers anyway. After eating three or four, he burped and tasted the gasoline on his breath. *They're treating us like dogs, throwing us their garbage.*

Rod resented the food even more after seeing what comprised the guerrillas' superior diet. On evenings when the hostages ate only rice, the kidnappers cooked a turkey or chicken for themselves. They had candy for themselves and blocks of hard peanut butter in plastic bags. Rod started counting the number of times he saw the guerrillas with Coca-Cola or Fantas, and stopped at fifty.

Before long, the hostages started to stink. They sweated constantly in the relentless daytime heat and huddled together at night during the chilly, evening rains. They couldn't bathe, and had no deodorant or soap. The one saving grace was that they all had body odour. No one had grounds to complain.

Rod longed for Jane's clean house. He would give anything to hear her nagging him to pick up the snowmobile parts he had piled in the living room. He began to scheme about ways to get home to her.

One evening, in the midst of a torrential thunderstorm that flooded the area underneath the tarpaulin shelter, Rod told the others he felt like running. He was sure he could get a serious head start—the weather was so awful the guerrillas hadn't ventured from their tents to check on their hostages.

"Next time it rains like this, I'm going to disappear into the trees," he said. "It's pouring so fucking hard no one will see me."

It was a hollow threat, just frustrated talk, mostly. But two minutes later, the guerrillas were at the hostages' shelter, shining their flashlights into the pipeliners' faces. For the next few hours, throughout the deluge, the guerrillas repeated their search every ten minutes.

It was as if they'd heard Rod's threat to run. *Is the tent bugged? It would be easy enough. All they'd have to do is hook a tiny microphone under one of the tree branches holding up the shelter. I wouldn't put it past them.*

The paranoia and trauma began to manifest itself in the hostages' dreams, especially Barney's. One morning, Barney told Rod about his previous evening's nightmares and the tales would send shivers down Rod's back.

In one dream, Barney was back in Edmonton and stumbled across the guerrillas in his local watering hole. He realized the kidnappers recognized him and walked over to talk with them. Barney convinced the guerrillas all was forgiven and lured them back to his apartment with the promise of loose women and *cervesas*. In his apartment, blood covered the walls from the floor to the ceiling, but the guerrillas didn't notice and when Barney began to hack them all to pieces with a machete, they were too surprised to run. Barney skinned them alive, buried them in his backyard and force-fed pieces of their flesh to a second round of guerrillas he enticed back to the apartment.

Finally, Rod had heard one too many of these lurid tales. The next time Barney said, "Hey, Rod, want to hear about another brutal dream I had last night?", Rod told him to fuck off and to keep his dreams to himself. Rod made a mental note to keep an eye on his friend. All the pipeliners were irritable and high-strung, but Barney was closer to the edge than any of them.

Cigarettes were the hostages' only escape, and they came only rarely. The guerrillas might give the eight pipeliners one or two smokes at supper time to split among themselves or Barney, Rod or somebody else would work up the courage to beg for one between meals. The cigarettes were treasured: They were part anti-depressant, part appetite-suppressant and the hostages got churlish and snappy when they needed a smoke and couldn't get one.

Because they were so tightly rationed, a strict rule applied to the cigarettes: one drag, then pass it along. Rod watched like a hawk as the prized smoke made its way down the line towards him. The rule was easier to enforce at night, when the orange glow of the cigarette brightened each time they inhaled.

One night, the protocol was broken. As all eight pipeliners shared a rare after-dinner cigarette under their tarp, Neil slipped in a quick second drag before passing it along. Colin caught him.

"You double-dragging son-of-a-bitch!" Colin said, pointing an accusing finger at Neil. "What the hell do you think you're doing?"

Neil snapped. Although Colin outweighed him by at least sixty pounds, Neil pounced on him, put him in a headlock and punched him in the head, arms and back. He wouldn't let go.

Colin hadn't seen the attack coming. "Get off me, Neil," he yelled. "Get off me!"

But Neil wouldn't stop pummelling Colin. The two yelled obscenities at each other, screams Rod was sure the guerrillas would hear. That made him nervous. "Smarten up, Neil," he hissed under his breath. "Get off him, now! You're going to get us all shot. Get off him!"

Immediately, six guerrillas burst into the tent, screaming in Spanish. They pried Neil off Colin. *Oh, man, we're dead. We are dead.*

But the guerrillas didn't punish them. In fact, Lario, the kidnapper who had lost his contact lens earlier in the jungle, seemed shaken by the United workers' fight.

"You two, friends," he said in a pleading voice. "Friends, friends, *no problemo.*"

His English was rough, but his message was clear: You guys don't fight each other, you help each other. You're in this together.

Amazingly, Lario appeared to fight back tears as he gave Colin and Neil another cigarette to calm their tempers. The jungle was making everyone—hostages and guerrillas—crazy.

Although Ander, Sabine, Maria and Jesus often slept in a separate tarpaulin shelter at night, Rod began to get to know—and develop mixed feelings for—his fellow captives. Rod liked and respected Maria and Jesus, the honeymooners from Bilbao, Spain. Jesus, a trim, bearded, quiet sort, revealed to Rod and the other men that he was a police officer in Spain. He snuck the pipeliners smokes from the dwindling stash he'd snatched from the tourists' van. Maria, a nurse with a mass of curly black hair, was a spirited, fiery woman who often stood up to the guerrillas when they served especially awful meals. The couple's honeymoon had been ruined, but their good humour made Rod's time in the jungle a little more endurable.

But Rod had no time for Ander, who whined constantly about the heavy backpacks the guerrillas forced them to carry. A small man, slight and lean, Ander was always asking for preferential treatment because of his size.

"You're big and strong. I am weak," Ander would tell Rod and the other pipeliners, as the sun beat down on their heads. "You should carry the bags."

Rod suspected Ander and Sabine, who knew more English than Maria and Jesus, were not doing a good job as translators. Sometimes, during breaks in marches or at meal times, they would carry on twenty-minute conversations with the guerrillas, yet return to the oil workers with little information. Rod didn't blame Ander and Sabine for being polite to the guerrillas; it would be unwise to be impertinent. But he felt frustrated at being kept out of the loop.

"What did they say?" Rod asked Ander after a particularly long chat with the captors. "When are they going to let us out of here? What's going on?"

But all Ander said was, "We're going to eat now," and Rod fumed, knowing they'd discussed a lot more than supper.

Rod sympathized with Colin at one point when his friend grew furious with Sabine for evading his questions after she talked with the kidnappers for more than forty-five minutes.

"What did they say?" Colin asked Sabine. "What were you talking about?"

Sabine just brushed him off: "Oh, it was nothing about you."

It enraged Rod, who was desperate to know when he could return home to his wife and daughter. He couldn't understand why Ander or Sabine would talk to the guerrillas for so long without sharing the details.

Ander did share one valuable, if predictable, bit of information: he, Sabine, Maria and Jesus would be released before the pipeliners. This confirmed what Rod had suspected from the beginning: The United men were the real targets here; Ander, Sabine, Maria and Jesus were mistakes.

Rod also tired of Ander's advice on how best to act in the jungle after he himself was gone. Ander encouraged the oil workers to eat as much as they could, no matter how poor the meals. That

74

would reduce the guerrillas' own food supply and make them weaker, leading to shorter marches, Ander reasoned.

Rod was happy that Barney, at least, got along well with Sabine. The rough-and-tumble Albertan pipeliner and the Belgian-born Canadian aid worker, two people from wildly different backgrounds, spent hours in the guerrilla encampments fending off their constant hunger by talking about the gourmet food and fine wine they would consume back in Canada. Sabine told Barney she'd bring him a pizza from a place in Quito the moment he was released.

Sabine spent much of her time in the jungle with a pen and paper she had among the belongings she took from the van. Rod figured she was writing a university thesis or a paper. She was educated, well-spoken and a proud Quebecer. She argued with the Alberta men about whether Quebec should secede from Canada to become an independent country.

Rod was uncomfortable with the subject of separation. *Why don't they just keep it to themselves? Albertans never bring it up. It's always the Quebecers who want to discuss it.*

Rod never challenged Sabine's views, but Colin was always up for a fight. He chastised Sabine for her notion that Quebec was the most beautiful part of Canada.

"What the hell are you talking about?" said Colin, the dictionary definition of the proud, indignant Albertan.

"I spent many years in university in Quebec," she replied. "It's so nice. It's clean. The people are great."

Sabine taunted Colin, asked him if it was true that Alberta was populated by right-wing rednecks.

Rod ground his teeth, but kept his mouth shut. *Separate, you bunch of free-loading bastards. Take the shirts on your backs and go. Just don't expect to take half the country with you.*

Even in the Ecuadorean jungle, a hemisphere away from the Péquiste movement's roots and the birthplace of Western Canadian alienation, the Quebec question had reared its ugly head. It was a truly Canadian moment.

Politics and Cigarettes The tensions between Rod and Ander and some of the men and Sabine, however, were niggling and inconsequential compared to the brewing discontent between the pipeliners and Barry, their boss. Before the capture, Rod respected Barry and considered him a friend from their days as acreage neighbours. Rod thought his boss was a touch quick with the odd harsh putdown or angry condemnation on the job site, but he appreciated that different men had different management styles. Rod was prepared to put up with Barry's attitude on the pipeline, but not in the jungle.

Barry's habit of swearing angrily at the guerrillas was the first thing that touched off Rod and the other United men. Many of the Canadians did swear at the guerrillas, who were unaware of the range and scope of English profanity. Often, when one of the kidnappers walked by the hostages, Grant or Barney would smile sweetly and say, "Hey, asshole!" or "Hi, fuckhead!" in a pleasant voice. The guards would look at them blankly. But when Barry swore at the kidnappers, it was different.

"Jesus Christ, you sons-of-bitches, feeding us this shit," he growled under his breath at mealtimes when a guerrilla handed over a bowl of scorched rice and beans. Rod worried Barry was going to get himself and everyone else killed. The guerrillas didn't know much English, but they weren't stupid. They must have understood "Jesus Christ," and even if they didn't, they could guess at Barry's sentiment from his tone and his body language.

Those weren't the only risks Barry took in the jungle. Often, when the hostages were ordered to sit quietly in a circle, Barry would remain standing or pace back and forth. The guerrillas seemed to cut him extra slack because he was the boss, but he was pushing his luck.

Barry's behaviour was especially risky on night marches, when the guerrillas were most tense. The group often walked all night to avoid the Ecuadorean army, which, judging from the two soldiers the guerrillas claimed to have stabbed in the neck, was closing in on them. Helicopters still flew over the jungle daily. At night, there was gunfire, presumably from soldiers on patrol.

It was obviously risky, but the group skulked past military checkpoints and through farmyards, sometimes getting so close to houses they could hear the sound of a radio playing. Dogs howled as they crept past.

But the guerrillas had excellent night vision and managed to move through the brush with little trouble or noise in the midnight black. The same could not be said for the hostages—they often tripped over fallen tree branches and crashed to the ground, or wandered perilously close to cliff sides that hung over thirty-metre drops. Some of the hostages, dazed with fear and fatigue, hallucinated on the night marches. Rod saw trees and animals where there were none, and bumped into the backs of the men walking ahead of him.

Rod marvelled at the ability of the guerrillas to spot potential hazards, even at night. He'd feel a whack on the shoulder, and a kidnapper would point to a leaf on the ground.

"No," the guerrilla would whisper, turning the leaf over slowly with the barrel of his gun. Sure enough, there would be a scorpion under the leaf, coiled and waiting to bite.

One night, in the middle of an excruciatingly long, spooky night march, the guerrillas told the hostages to remain silent on a hillside while they plotted their next move. But Barry kept talking, muttering about the insanity of walking through the pitch-black jungle. One of the kidnappers passed a blunt message to Barry through the Spaniards: "Warn him that if he tries anything, if he talks, if he does anything—dead," the guerrilla said, emphasizing his threat with the universal throat-slitting gesture.

After conferring on the hill for more than three hours, the guerrillas told the group it was time to *vamoose*. They tied Barry and Rod together with a five-metre rope so Rod could keep the older man in line.

Three guerrillas led the way with machine guns. Rod and Barry followed walking side-by-side because of their leash. The others walked in single file behind them.

"Don't talk to him," the guerrillas told Rod. "He's bad, bad, *malo, malo.*"

Barry tried to complain to Rod a few times, but Rod would have none of it. "We're not talking, Barry," he said. "We're not talking." The men trudged on in silence, Rod seething at the spot Barry had put him in.

The simmering tension finally exploded a couple of mornings later. Barry, always a stickler for tidiness, demanded that the other United workers clean a mess by the hostages' tent. He also wanted a nearby log cut down and moved so ants wouldn't infest their cramped sleeping area.

These orders—and that's what they were, orders—were the last straw. The other men turned on him.

"Get off your fat fucking ass and do it yourself," one of the pipeliners said. "If you're sharing in the responsibility, share in the work detail." They tore Barry down for being lazy, for bullying them and for jeopardizing their safety by talking back to the guerrillas.

It was an ugly scene, full of hostility and recrimination. Rod felt sorry for Barry. It must be tough to be the boss and then have something like this happen, he thought. There is no human resources manual describing how to manage employees in the event of a hostage-taking.

But something had to be said to Barry, or this could turn into a full-fledged brawl much uglier than the little scrap between Colin and Neil over smokes.

Eventually, the men hashed it out, and the ultimate message was clear: Barry might have been the boss on the job, but he sure as hell wasn't the boss in the jungle.

"We're all in this together, Barry," Rod said. "From now on, everything will be a decided by majority vote."

Barry didn't agree, but he relented. Democracy reigned. Votes would be held on everything from divvying up the rationed cigarettes to the appropriate times to ask Ander and Sabine to pump the guerrillas for information.

It was a turning point for the men. They realized they had to pull together. None of the pipeliners would ever be candidates to run a seminar on expressing your feelings, but they knew they had to lean on one another if they wanted to make it out alive.

Like most buddies, the pipeliners had relationships based on work and partying and automobiles, not on confiding their feelings to one another. But, slowly, the men started to open up.

Leonard, like Steven Brent, was quiet on marches and in the guerrillas' encampments, deep within his own terror-filled thoughts. But one day he launched into conversation with Rod about his dreams.

Leonard's cousin, a medicine man on his Navajo reservation in Utah, had told Leonard about the significance of his dreams. Unlike Barney's nightmares, Technicolor affairs where the bullets and the blood flew, Leonard's dreams were full of people who meant a lot to him, people he hadn't seen for a long time or friends and relatives who had passed away. Leonard told Rod his dreams meant he'd get out of the jungle and return to Utah to see his loved ones again.

These dreams were rare moments of serenity for Leonard, who otherwise appeared to worry almost as much as Barney.

"Rod, what do you think, man? Are we going to get out of here alive?" he asked one day.

"Yeah, of course we're getting out of here," Rod replied.

"It's not looking good, man," Leonard said, shaking his head. "Look at my feet."

Rod watched in horror as Leonard peeled off his damp boots. His toenails had turned blood-black and were starting to rip off. Leonard's feet were rotting from hours spent walking through boggy swamps and thick mud.

All the men were in bad shape. Several had fungal infections around their groins—crotch rot, Rod called it—from dampness, constant walking and lack of bathing. Barney scratched his legs and groin until they bled. Rod stopped wearing his only pair of underwear because it made the chafing worse.

The odd food and questionable water gave the hostages stomach aches, terrible gas and indigestion that wouldn't go away. Barry, who rarely talked to the other men after the fight about his behaviour, yearned for a convenience store so he could buy a tube of Rolaids.

The guerrillas seemed to delight in grossing out their captives with the food. One day the female kidnapper boiled a monkey for the hostages. She carried a bowl over to Rod with the monkey's skull in it—the hair had been boiled clean off the bone.

Rod couldn't imagine eating it, but thought the skull might make a cool souvenir for his daughter.

"For me, for me?" Rod asked the woman kidnapper. "I take that home? I take that *casa*?"

But the woman obviously misunderstood Rod, thinking he wanted to eat some of it. Taking a dagger from her pouch, she hacked through the top of the skull until the slimy brains slipped out. She put some in her mouth, chewed, and smiled.

Rod gagged and thought he was going to vomit right there. It looked exactly like the diagrams of the human brain he'd studied years ago in science class.

The woman scooped the brains into a bowl and passed them around. Rod politely refused but some of the other guys were hungry enough to try it. Neil, who hated the jalapeno peppers but ate just about anything else, seemed to enjoy it.

The woman laughed at Rod. She quickly picked up on the fact that he didn't have the stomach for various types of jungle fare. On marches where the two of them walked closely together, she'd grab a termite nest on a branch, crack it open and lick the larvae right from the nest. She pinched the heads off the live insects and sucked out their insides. Bugs crawled over her lips when she turned and offered Rod some.

Once he agreed but it was a big mistake. The larvae were mostly tasteless but their smooth, wet texture made him gag.

When the hostages weren't eating jungle insects, they were avoiding their attacks. The bugs seemed especially malevolent towards like Leonard, who was always suffering from bites.

Still, nothing prepared him for the night of the ant attack.

The men were sleeping on the ground under a tarp suspended between two trees. It was the middle of the night, a rare evening off between night marches. Rod and Leonard lay next to each other.

Suddenly, Leonard sat bolt upright in bed, jumped to his feet and started screaming. Rod leapt up, bewildered and groggy.

"What the hell is going on?" Rod asked, disoriented and unsure about exactly where he was, still caught halfway in the no-man's land between restless sleep and heightened awareness. Though Leonard was only a few feet away, the jungle dark was so inky black and pure that Rod could not see him. "What's going on, Leonard?" he ventured.

"They're biting me, Rod!" Leonard screeched as he flailed about, hitting his arms, his legs, any body part he could reach. "They're biting me!"

The guerrillas standing guard outside the hostages' lean-to, rushed in. One shone a flashlight on Leonard's whirling torso. Immediately Rod saw what Leonard was screaming about: thousands of tiny red ants scurried over his body, sinking their tiny pincers into his skin. Rod's eyes flashed to the log Leonard had leaned back against to help him sleep. The ants must have crawled out of there.

"Do something, guys!" Leonard yelled, but all Rod and the others could do was watch helplessly.

One of the guerrillas sprinted to a nearby tent, which served as the camp's kitchen, snatched a container of Coleman's camping fuel, and tossed it over Leonard's skin. Rod shivered. The fuel would drive away the ants, but its sting would hurt as bad as their bites.

Rod tried to comfort Leonard, who was still near hysterics, as he surveyed the damage: Leonard's body was covered in angry red welts and he reeked of fuel.

The guerrillas tried to calm everybody down with a couple of cigarettes. Leonard flopped back on the ground, as far away from the log as possible, still shaking.

Rod and the others joked weakly about the incident, but couldn't sleep. No one knew when the next attack would come.

Rod had only one weapon to combat the wretched, soul-destroying surroundings—constant conversation with the other men about Edmonton, about home. They talked for hours about their plans, their snowmobiles and trucks and motorcycles, their wives and girlfriends.

When he sat with Leonard, around the nightly fire or under the tarpaulin shelter, Rod steered their talk in any direction but ants. Leonard, an avid hunter, pined for the brand new rifle he'd left behind in Utah. He'd bought it just before the Ecuador trip and hadn't fired a shell from it. He couldn't wait to try it out, though he doubted he'd be home in time for hunting season. He was jealous of his brother Wayne, who was surely out every weekend, bombing around in Leonard's truck, hunting for deer.

Rod teased Leonard: "Don't worry, man. Wayne probably has your rifle, and he's probably using your tags."

Leonard glared at Rod. "Nope, he wouldn't do that. It's a brand new gun."

"Oh yeah, Wayne would do it," Rod laughed.

Often, the men talked about their families. Colin, especially, spoke fondly of his wife Karen, things they'd done together, trips they'd taken, the moment he knew he was in love with her.

Colin talked incessantly about his children. He told Rod he wanted to take his son to Edmonton Oilers hockey games. He wanted to play with his daughters more, too, and take the whole gang on a camping trip in the motorhome to Lake Mead near Las Vegas.

Rod thought about the renovations he wanted to do to his house. He planned to put hardwood in the bedroom, tear out a couple of walls and repaint. They were humdrum, workaday plans, but thinking about them helped him withstand all the drudgery and uncertainty, the fear and the night marches.

Family talk never failed to lift Colin's spirits, but it often depressed Rod, reminding him he might never see Jane and Krissy again. Once, when Colin was in the midst of a reverie about Karen and the kids, Rod left the shelter, knelt in the jungle dirt and stared up at the sky. He didn't want the other men to see how desperate he was.

Rod fretted about how Jane would explain his absence to Krissy. He hoped she wouldn't scare her, would let her think he'd be coming home soon. He couldn't bear the thought of Krissy growing up without him.

He'd never felt more helpless in his life. But he willed himself to stay strong. He could sense that some of the other pipeliners— Barney, especially—were following his lead, picking up their emotional cues from him, looking to him to keep up their morale. If he cracked, they'd crack too. But if he could keep it together, they'd all have a better shot of going home sane.

On September 21, Day 11 of their captivity, Rod had no choice but to think about his family as the guerrillas gave him a surprise chance to send a message to Jane and Krissy in Edmonton.

The guerrillas announced that Ander would be released with a list of radio frequencies and codenames the pipeliners' employer could use to contact them. Ander was obviously thrilled as he packed his bags. But before splitting from the group, he asked the kidnappers if he could take a picture of the hostages to prove to their families they were still healthy and alive. But the guerrillas refused. Instead they allowed Ander to pass around a few sheets of paper so the hostages could scribble notes to their loved ones.

The guerrillas instructed the men to sit in a line on the ground as they wrote. Keep it short, they said. And nothing about food, the conditions, their whereabouts or any description of the kidnappers.

The hostages were forced to share two pieces of paper between eight people. It amounted to a quarter-page each, a half-page if they used both sides. There was only one pen, and the guerrillas wanted the messages written immediately. They had precious little time to collect their thoughts.

Ander had given the pipeliners grief over the past days, but Rod privately saluted him for the quick thinking that led to the hostages' chance to write to their families. That said, writing his letter felt like picking at a raw wound. It was the most difficult thing he had ever done. He was confronted with an immense range of emotions—love for his family, desperation at their situation, fear, euphoria, loneliness. All the men cried except Barry, though Rod suspected his hard-nosed boss teared up when he had his back to the group.

Rod's letter read: "*Dear Jane and Krissy,*

Love you very much and miss you very much. We are all OK. Waiting to come home soon.

Love, Rod Dunbar."

It was not especially eloquent, but it was all he could think of to put down.

Rod could see that Grant, especially, was having a tough time trying to tell his family what they meant to him on a tiny square of paper. He sobbed quietly as he wrote his letter to his parents.

Struggling to maintain his own composure, Rod wanted to make Grant feel better, but found no words to comfort him.

"What's wrong?" he asked, knowing as soon as the words left his mouth it was a dumb question to ask.

Tears streaming down his face, Grant kept his head down. Rod said nothing more.

Finally, Grant looked up. "What the hell do you mean, what's wrong?" he said.

Rod gave his friend a playful kick. Grant mustered a weak laugh. Joking around was how the men dealt best with adversity in the jungle. Being serious made things worse.

The guerrillas ordered Ander to translate the pipeliners' letters into Spanish to make sure they gave no clues about the hostages' whereabouts. Once satisfied, they ordered the others to *vamoose*, leaving Ander with a handful of guerrillas to accompany him back to civilization.

Despite the tension Ander had caused, Rod still hoped the little Spaniard would reach civilization safely, and get the radio frequencies securely in the hands of the negotiators. *Now that Ander's free maybe we're all one step closer to being free.*

———

Ander and his guerrilla guards walked for five days and nights until reaching the outskirts of Lago Agrio, where the Spaniard was finally cut loose on September 26.

Filthy, exhausted and hungry, Ander scurried to a local aid agency office. From there he called his family, his fiancée and his co-workers at ALER. Then he boarded a plane for Quito. Staff at the ALER radio station reacted with jubilation.

Ander told the media Sabine, Maria and Jesus would be released in the coming weeks. It was only a matter of time.

"The only thing I can say for sure is that [the guerrillas] are interested in the oil workers," he told more than 100 journalists at a packed news conference the next day in Quito. "The rest of us aren't of interest to them."

Looking pale and gaunt, Ander described what he called "our tragic adventure." He said the guerrillas sent no ransom demands, just a request that indigenous people and the environment be better treated by big business and by government.

He said the kidnappers treated the hostages decently, but that they walked constantly and lived on a diet of snakes, ants, leaves and roots.

"There were logs, broken trees, snakes that came close to biting us and mountains of insects," he said. "Curiously, no one became ill, no one broke a leg.

"We would walk two hours, then rest for half an hour, then walk for half an hour and rest for ten minutes. We had no idea which way was north, south, east or west."

Journalists were frantic to know who the kidnappers were. FARC? ELN? Paramilitaries? Common bandits?

Ander said he didn't know who the kidnappers were, but he detected Colombian, Ecuadorean and Peruvian accents, lending credence to the theory that the guerrillas were not FARC, but a well-organized band of criminals.

Ander said he believed he'd been freed in order to reassure their families that the hostages were fine. The oil workers were bearing up well considering the circumstances, he said. His sister Maria and brother-in-law Jesus were doing fine, too. But, although Sabine was physically fit, she seemed insecure in the jungle and was having trouble handling the emotional strain.

Ander told them he hoped the Ecuadorean army would fail in its efforts to find the kidnappers and the hostages.

"I don't believe they will find them. I personally hope they don't find them. That could be the most dangerous situation."

Enfermo

SIX DAYS AFTER Ander Mimenza was released into the steamy wilds surrounding Lago Agrio, the guerrillas made contact with the outside world. Hostage negotiators picked up a signal on a noisy, static-filled ham radio channel at a heavily guarded safe house in a gated community a forty-minute drive outside of Quito. There were five men in the room that night: two negotiators from the Miami-based Ackerman group; FBI agents Dennis Braiden and George Kazynski; and Sgt. Gord Black of the RCMP's E-Division internal unit in Vancouver.

As had been their habit the previous five nights, the men listened to a local music program until 6 p.m., then tuned their radio to one of the frequencies the guerrillas gave in their message to Ander. The ham radio channels had code names corresponding to South American countries—Brazil, Peru, Venezuela. The previous five nights, the men waited patiently on the predetermined "Brazil" channel, but heard nothing except the oscillating wash of white noise. But on this night, shortly after 6 p.m., through Brazil's squelch and the static, the negotiators heard a voice, disembodied and faint, but unmistakably that of one of the guerrillas.

"*Tio Conejo. Tio Conejo,*" it said. *Tio Conejo*—Uncle Rabbit— was the negotiators' code name.

"*Tio Conejo. Tio Conejo. Abuelo. Abuelo.*" *Abuelo*—Grandfather— was the kidnappers' code name.

Apart from the ham radio's hiss, the safe house was silent. At the word "Abuelo," Dennis Braiden and Gord Black locked eyes and nodded. Their communication was silent, though it spoke volumes. After days of waiting, they were up and running.

Gord Black received the order to fly to Ecuador in late September, just as he was preparing to attend a conference on hostage negotiating at the Justice Institute of British Columbia. When his pager went off, showing a number from RCMP headquarters in Ottawa, Gord felt a wave of adrenaline wash over him. *This is it. This is the one.*

At the time, Gord was the only RCMP officer in Canada trained to negotiate with terrorists. The year before, RCMP brass in Ottawa determined the force lacked the ability to deal effectively with terrorists, and sent Gord to take a special course in London, England. One of the things he'd learned from the British negotiators who'd developed their tactics during hostage-taking situations in Afghanistan and in Chechnya, was how to negotiate "in the blind" over ham radio. This was precisely the method he'd be forced to use in Ecuador.

Immediately after returning the page, Gord boarded a plane to Ottawa that afternoon, and left the nation's capital for Ecuador within twenty-four hours. While in Ottawa, he was outfitted with extensive jungle gear, given several vaccinations for equatorial diseases including yellow fever and malaria, and taken to several briefings.

That night, Gord called his family and friends. All were distraught to hear he would be participating in such a dangerous situation. Gord shared his loved ones' fear of the unknown, but was eager to apply what he'd learned in Europe to saving Canadian lives.

The following evening, September 21, he landed in Quito. Back home in Canada, it was the beginning of autumn but it was perpetual spring in Ecuador's capital. He was greeted at the airport by

Jaime Sebastian, an RCMP constable stationed in Bogota, Colombia, and by two members of UNASE, the Ecuadorean National Police's anti-kidnapping and extortion unit. The local cops treated Gord to a trip to a Quito restaurant, where he was honoured with a serving of rat's intestine, a local delicacy. Gord, hoping to make a good impression on his new colleagues, ate it with a smile.

The following week was a whirlwind of meetings with Ambassador Kneale, intelligence gathering with the UNASE men, and planning sessions with his co-negotiators from the FBI and the Ackerman group. The ground rules for the negotiations were these: The Ackerman men, United Pipeline's direct representatives, would speak to the guerrillas once contact was made, and Gord, Braiden and Kazynski would advise and consult with them on tactics. Although the predominant feeling among Ecuadorean and Canadian authorities was that the guerrillas were members of FARC, Gord and the other negotiators agreed they wouldn't pigeonhole the kidnappers' identities. It was too early in the kidnapping to be that definitive. Furthermore, if the negotiators didn't peg the guerrillas, their minds would be clear of stereotypes and more able to react objectively to the kidnappers' demands. The team spent hours discussing contingencies, psychology and strategy. On September 26, when Ander was released with the radio frequencies, their work began in earnest.

"*Tio Conejo. Tio Conejo. Abuelo. Abuelo,*" said the guerrilla over the ham radio.

The reception was terrible—the modulation was way off—but one of the Ackerman negotiators grabbed the radio's transmitter and, in Spanish, confirmed he was Tio Conejo and that he could hear the guerrilla.

"Your family is OK," the guerrilla said, confirming that the pipeliners were alive and well. The Ackerman rep said that was good news.

The guerrilla's next words were the ones the negotiators were itching to hear: After a long pause, the guerrilla said his group was demanding $20 million U.S. for the pipeliners' release. The

Ackerman reps had been authorized by United Pipeline officials to make a counter-offer of $1 million, but had decided to make this offer later because they did not want to let the guerrillas know United was prepared to respond immediately with money. Instead the Ackerman rep replied that Tio Conejo understood Abuelo's demand and then made arrangements to speak again the following night. The whole exchange took less than four minutes.

Once it was over, Gord and the FBI agents were elated. It didn't matter whether the guerrillas were asking for $20 million or twenty cents—the important thing was that negotiations were finally underway. After three weeks of mystery and radio silence, at last they would be able to help the pipeliners.

———

Abuelo told Tio Conejo the "family" was alive, but in truth, by the end of September, the hostages wished they were dead.

The punishing regimen of night walks, bad food, three weeks without a bath, insect bites, blisters and cramped sleeping arrangements—all took an enormous toll. The pipeliners were shedding weight like jungle snakes shed their skins.

After releasing Ander, the kidnappers put several kilometres between themselves and the freed Spaniard, setting up a longer-term camp. By now the dreadful conditions of the previous days caught up with the pipeliners and several came down with minor and major sicknesses.

Although Barry kept mostly to himself after his bitter argument with the other men, he complained to the others that his stomach ached. Nothing serious, he said, just a bad bout of indigestion that wouldn't go away, a constant churning from eating terrible food.

Still, Rod was worried. It seemed odd that Barry, one of the toughest, strongest pipeliners in the business, would grouse about a mere bellyache. He was too proud to complain about minor pains.

I hope it's not his appendix. If it is, he's a goner. There's no way we could get him to a doctor in time. The guerrillas would probably shoot him or leave him behind to die on his own. They wouldn't care. It'd be one less mouth to feed.

Barney, too, had concerns, but about his asthma. Though the jungle's high humidity actually helped his lungs, the arduous marches certainly didn't. Speaking through Ander and Sabine, he'd repeatedly demanded new inhalers from the guerrillas, but to no avail.

Asthmatics who carry inhalers know intuitively how many puffs they have left. The morning the pipeliners were captured, Barney shook his inhaler and estimated he had twenty-five days of medication remaining. Now, they were on Day 18 with no replacement inhaler in sight.

Barney walked up to a guerrilla and shook the near-empty puffer in his face.

"Seven days to my death if you don't get me one of these," Barney said. "Seven more days."

The guerrilla understood, but shook his head. It would take at least seven days to find one, maybe longer, he said in Spanish to Ander and Sabine.

The translated response enraged Barney. "I've told you all along," he said. "No inhaler, I die."

A few days later, in a small miracle, the guerrillas actually produced an inhaler for Barney. But, unfortunately, it wasn't full strength, just some bargain-basement puffer with one-quarter the necessary medication. Barney took his old inhaler and the new one back to the guerrilla and held them in the air, one in each hand.

"Four puffs from this," he said, pointing to the new puffer, "equals one from this," pointing to the old.

The guerrilla shrugged and, through the interpreters, instructed Barney to use the stronger inhaler when he had difficulty breathing. Otherwise, the weaker one would have to suffice.

Enfermo

The hostages all worried about Barney but, as September bled into October, their focus shifted to Rod.

Rod could scarcely comprehend the variety of garbage he'd been given to eat since the capture, the burnt rice, the still-warm monkey brains, the oozing insect eggs and the gasoline-soaked crackers. But a fresh horror stared back at Rod one suppertime when he peered into the bowl he shared with Barry and Barney. In the bowl was a fatty, pink pig's head, still bristly with hair.

Rod had seen the guerrillas bring the slaughtered pig into camp. He presumed they'd either stolen it from a farmer's yard or bought it from an ally who lived in one of the nearby villages. The kidnappers hacked the animal into sections with their machetes, then separated these into two piles—meat for themselves, skin and entrails for the hostages. The guerrillas salted the pork, and except for that night's dinner, stored it in burlap sacks.

After boiling it, one of the guerrillas dumped the pig's head into Rod's bowl, and the Canadian nearly retched. He picked at the face, searching for anything edible among the clumps of hair and the eye and snout holes. Just then something caught his eye, and he looked up to see tiny lights shimmering through the trees where the guerrillas were eating their portions. Rod realized that the kidnappers were flicking their Bic lighters, not to light cigarettes, but to singe the remaining hair from the pork.

I wish I had a lighter, Rod thought miserably to himself, turning his attention back to the pig's head. He flipped it over in the bowl and spied a piece of meat on the inside. He bit into it but gagged and spat it out. It was gristly and, despite the salt, tasted rotten. Although he'd eaten little more than child portions of mostly inedible jungle fare for the past twenty days, he was too revolted to try any more.

"No, I can't do this," he said, passing the boiled face over to Barry and Barney. "I can't eat that."

Without waiting to see whether his companions would eat the head, he walked back to the hostages' tarpaulin shelter. As he lay down in his hammock, Rod felt his throat begin to swell and close. His head throbbed. He could feel something coming on, but thought he could sleep it off. He dozed on his back, tucking his knees into his chest to fight the familiar beginning waves of nausea.

When he awoke at dawn the next morning, Rod was near-delirious with fever. Bent over at the waist, he walked shakily out of the tent, where several guerrillas were on guard. Rod pointed to a section of trees, signalling that he wanted to use the group's makeshift latrine, but managed only a few steps before falling hard on his knees. After a furious fit of vomiting, the dry heaves began, so hard he thought his ribs would break.

Colin, trained in Canada as an emergency medical technician, ran over to put pressure on Rod's ribs. Following Colin's lead, Rod wrapped his own arms tightly around his chest. He stopped vomiting. Colin murmured words of concern. Rod saw his friend's lips move but couldn't hear him: it was as if the ferocity of his vomiting had momentarily deafened him.

"Can I get you anything, buddy?" Colin said. "Water, anything?"

Rod was too far gone even to acknowledge him.

He staggered back to the tent. Breakfast that morning was rice and more of the pork from the night before. As if, Rod thought. He couldn't even look at the food without retching again. Everything, even the water, gathered from nearby streams and stored in two-litre pop bottles, tasted like the pig's head—greasy, salty and rancid.

As the day wore on his illness grew worse. Constant diarrhea soiled him. Whenever he moved his head, his eyes bulged and rattled in their sockets and he sprayed vomit over the side of the hammock. Colin tried to get him to drink, but soon after Rod took a sip of water, he was dizzily rolling out of his tent to vomit it back up.

"You've got to eat, Rod," Colin told him. "You've got to feed the machine."

Rod couldn't. He thought it was better to deprive his sickness rather than fuel it.

"I know my body," he told Colin weakly. "I know what I'm like when I'm sick. If I starve myself, I get better quicker. Leave me alone and I'll rest it off."

The guerrillas kept their weapons trained on the hostages, watching stonily as Rod battled through the nausea and fever. They offered no medicine or aid of any kind. *They don't give a shit. If I die, they'll haul my carcass out to the road or just bury it and tell the authorities where to pick it up.*

Rod, at least, had the other hostages looking out for him, even Barry, who had personal reasons to keep his distance. Barry, who shared a blanket with Rod, made sure it covered him at all times and comforted Rod as best he could.

"You're going to be OK, you're going to be OK," Barry told him, as the sweat rolled down Rod's pale face and he tried to kick the blanket away. "We'll get you out of this dogshit hole."

But by sunset, Rod was not so sure. He felt doomed, like he had no energy left to battle whatever raged inside him. He could do little but reflect on his life.

He thought of his mother Hilda back in Edmonton, who still babied him and bought him clothes. She had health problems and had lost several family members in recent years. Her own mother, Rod's grandmother, wasn't doing well. He contemplated how his family would react if they learned Rod had died of food poisoning or malaria while being held hostage by strange, violent men 4,000 kilometres from home. The news will kill them, he thought.

He curled his knees to his chest in the hammock and tried to recall happier memories. Christmas Eve, 1989 immediately came to mind—the day he asked Jane to marry him. Rod was always like an excited child at Christmas, insisting they all rip open their gifts the night before the big day. This Christmas Eve, he and Jane were at his mother's house and had already torn the wrapping off more than half their gifts.

Later that night, alone in the living room, Rod gestured to a tiny present high in the tree's branches: a single bulb from an egg carton. "You might as well open that one, too, Jane," he said. Inside was a diamond engagement ring.

Four years later Krissy was born. Typically, he was away from home on a job near Swan Hills, a bush town northwest of Edmonton, when he got the call from Jane. It was still a month before her due date, but she was going into labour.

The drive between Edmonton and Swan Hills was 250 kilometres, most of it on rutted two-lane blacktop, but Rod floored his pickup and made the journey in just under ninety minutes. Jane swore she heard Rod squeal up to the curb from the maternity ward in Edmonton's Misericordia Hospital.

The delivery had complications. Krissy, a month premature, stopped breathing twice after the birth, but the doctors quickly revived her. Later, Rod held the baby in his arms and cried. Doctors had told them Jane would never be able to have children, yet here they were, with their very own daughter. Krissy's tiny hand gripped Rod's thumb as he held her.

Suddenly Rod's daydream was interrupted—another dizzy spell, another wrenching wave of nausea, bad enough to make him pray for his life.

Rod never was one to have words with God. For fourteen years, he'd wrestled with steel pipe in deep gouges in the earth to make a good life for his family. The way Rod saw it, he had no one to thank for that life, not God, not anyone.

But now he was trapped like a sick animal on the other side of *Enfermo* the world with no way to turn. For the first time in his life, he prayed.

"Please, God, don't let me perish in this way, in this shit, in this filth. Please look after my family. Please let me get home to them," he murmured, almost silently, to himself.

He thought again of Krissy, of her tomboy ways, of how she always hunted him down in the house or yard to hug him before she went to sleep, and added a final line to his prayer.

"Please, God, don't let her grow up without a father."

Some ancient, ingrained survival mechanism kicked in during the night, and Rod awoke the next day, just as feverish and out-of-it as before. Maria took pity on Rod and asked if there was anything she could do.

"I need a doctor," Rod gasped. "I'm going to die here if I don't get a doctor."

Maria jogged over to the guerrilla commander and demanded he seek medical attention for Rod. Maria was not scared of the guerrillas; if anything, they were a little frightened of her. "*Enfermo*," she said. "He is sick. He needs a doctor."

The guerrilla commander said it wasn't possible. They couldn't risk being discovered by bringing in help from the outside.

Maria blasted the captors for the appalling conditions and the rancid food. Not only did they need medical attention for Rod, they needed more water and medicine.

The head guerrilla considered this, and finally relented. He ordered one of his underlings to give Rod what basic over-the-counter remedies they had in the camp. The junior guerrillas fetched Alka-Seltzer with water and lemon, Pepto-Bismol and a tablet of Anacin. That would have to do.

Rod figured taking Alka-Seltzer for what ailed him was like treating cancer with Tylenol, but it was all he had. He managed to sit up and swallow the weak drugs. He slept.

Amazingly, he started to improve the next day. His strength came back slowly and he could actually hold water down without throwing it back up again. His fever stopped spiking and then faded altogether.

Whether it was the meagre medicine or that the bug had simply run its course, Rod was better.

Maybe it was the praying that did it, he thought.

———————

Half a world away in Edmonton, Jane Dunbar lay naked on the cold bathroom floor, her hand pressed tight to her forehead. With all the strength she could summon from her spent body, she pulled herself to her knees, tottered grimly over the toilet bowl, and threw up.

She fell back on the floor, and lay there shaking in the dark. The lights were off; Jane had left them that way on purpose. Turned on, they were like spikes, stabbing at her eyes.

Jane managed to heave herself into the near-scalding tubful of water she'd managed to draw before collapsing on the tile floor.

It was another blinding migraine. It had hit the day before, starting with the awful foreshadowing tension in her neck, moving up the back of her head before settling behind her eyes. An observer, looking closely, could see her temples expand and contract with every heartbeat.

The only way Jane knew to ease the pain was to alternate between the boiling bath and the chilly floor. She'd battled migraines all her life. They'd come, suddenly, like summer thunderstorms or winter blizzards, once or twice a month. But now that Rod was gone and might never come back, Jane hardly went a day without one. She slept in the bathroom some nights, her head close to the toilet in case the overwhelming nausea hit.

She did what she could to take her mind off Rod. One night, she drove Krissy to her best friend's house for a sleepover and returned home looking forward to a rare night of peace and quiet.

Enfermo But just as she began to read, she felt the telltale signs of a headache coming on, starting with the taut feeling in her neck. She phoned a friend, hoping it might clear her head, but Jane's friend could sense something was wrong. She asked Jane how she was really doing, how she was really coping.

A pain shot through Jane's chest. Her heart racing, she burst into tears, said a hurried goodbye and got off the phone.

Ever since Rod was taken, Jane cried daily, but they were tears of anger and frustration—anger at the men who took her husband, frustration at the company for not doing enough to protect him.

These tears were different. She couldn't stop them. She screamed and cried, her breath shallow as she struggled to get air back into her lungs. Her head pounded, her heart raced and the sharp pain in her chest panicked her.

Jane phoned her mother in tears and told her what was happening. "Can you drive to the hospital?" her mom asked. "Yes, I think so," she replied. Misericordia, the same hospital where Krissy was born, was only a few blocks away.

"Call us when you get there and we'll come meet you."

Jane hung up the phone, still crying uncontrollably. She could barely see through her tears as she drove to the hospital and continued to bawl as she approached the admitting desk.

"I've got pains in my chest, my head is pounding and my hands won't stop shaking," she sobbed.

Nurses rushed her to a private room, bypassing the queue of people in the waiting room. She sat on the cot, still crying.

A doctor appeared. "What happened?" he asked. "What put you in this state?"

Jane told him she was the wife of one of the seven Edmonton pipeline workers held hostage in Ecuador. He understood right away, checked her pulse and gave her painkillers and pills to slow down her racing heart.

"It's an anxiety attack," the doctor said. "You're not going home by yourself."

Jane's parents drove her home. She collapsed into bed, physically and emotionally exhausted.

Jane drifted off to sleep, still in a haze from the painkillers, but not before telling herself that Krissy wouldn't be allowed to go on sleepovers again until Rod came home. She couldn't stand to be alone again.

Journalists called Jane endlessly to ask her reaction to the new developments in Ecuador. Sometimes they showed up unannounced at her door. At the time, little was known about the men who'd been taken hostage, and reporters repeatedly sought comment from family members.

One morning, Jane's doorbell rang. She opened the door without thinking, only to have a TV camera shoved in her face.

"No comment," she said wearily, but the station ran the clip anyway. Her aunt from Regina phoned that night to say she saw "Janie" in her housecoat on the news.

Great. People all over the country are seeing me at my absolute finest.

Most reporters were polite and understanding when she told them she couldn't talk. She understood they were just doing their jobs; they respected her right to refuse comment. But one reporter, from an upstart Edmonton television station called A-Channel, pressured her.

"What gives you the right to keep this information to yourself?" the man asked brusquely when Jane refused an on-camera interview.

"I beg your pardon," Jane replied, shocked that someone would speak to her that way.

"Don't you feel people should know about this?"

Jane slammed down the phone. The nerve, she thought.

Though none of the hostages' immediate families spoke to media, reporters still tried to unearth details about the men. They cold-called anyone who shared the hostages' last names and pumped them for information.

Enfermo

Jane's jaw dropped a few days after the capture when she opened the *Edmonton Sun* and read a story that quoted John Scheelar, Barney's nineteen-year-old cousin.

"Brant's a tough guy," John told the *Sun.* "I just hope he doesn't do anything rash. This is very shocking. I put it in the back of my head most of the time, but when it comes out I just hope Brant gets out safely."

Another cousin, who asked not to be named, told the paper she worried about Brant's stubborn, independent streak.

"Brant is a leader and he might try something, so we're a little bit scared for him," she said.

These were exactly the kinds of comments United had warned the families not to make. *What will happen if the guerrillas read this? Will they kill Barney in order to eliminate a potential troublemaker?*

Barney's brother Sean phoned the day the story ran. His voice quavered as he apologized to Jane on behalf of the family.

"I'm so sorry, Jane," he said. "We don't even really know John. He met Barney maybe a few times as a kid. That's it."

"Don't worry about it, Sean," Jane told him. "It's already out there. There's nothing you can do. I know it wasn't you."

The families continued to meet at Edmonton's east-end Holiday Inn every two or three weeks. Jane felt compelled to go, but she hated the meetings. At home she tried to pretend Rod was just away on a job somewhere, but at the meetings her fantasy world was shattered. Rod could be starving, sick, injured or dead. No one knew.

Ken Foster repeated that last fact at the meetings like a mantra.

"We don't know what's going on down there," he said. "We can't tell you anything more. That's all we can say."

Jane hated those words almost as much as the men who took her husband. She rolled her eyes every time she heard them. *They must know more. They're hiding it from us, because they don't want us to know how bad things are.*

Enfermo

Ed Leonard, the Canadian held hostage by FARC until his boss, Norbert Reinhart, switched places with him, visited the families at one of the meetings. Leonard described the conditions he'd experienced in the Colombian jungle. He'd eaten good food and played cards with his captors. They gave him soap, tooth-paste, beer, clean underwear, and even sent a nurse to visit him when he was ill.

The stories heartened Jane, although she didn't like one of the tales Leonard told. During a card game with the guerrillas, he play-fully chastised his opponent for cheating. The guerrilla jumped up and jammed the barrel of his machine gun in Leonard's face.

Some people at the meeting laughed, but Jane was sickened by the idea of poor-sport guerrillas with an arsenal of machine guns.

Leonard also told the families about a night walk when he lost his footing on a cliff and almost fell, but caught himself on a tree root sticking out of the ground. It was a scenario that hadn't occurred to Jane. *What if Rod fell and broke his leg? Would they shoot him in the head and leave his body to be eaten by some wild animal? What if the guerrillas decided the Canadians were too much trouble and shot them all to cut their losses?*

On September 26, word reached Edmonton that the guerrillas had released Ander Mimenza, one of the Spanish ecotourists taken hostage with the pipeliners. Jane was ecstatic; it gave her hope that Rod was still alive. She watched Ander's press conference on TV, eager to hear details about the men who kidnapped Rod and the environment he was living in.

Ander said the hostages were being treated well by their captors. The guerrillas didn't scream or threaten them. They were all alive. On hearing these last words, Jane's spirits soared.

Enfermo But then a reporter at the press conference asked Ander what the hostages were eating. Tree roots, leaves, insects, ants and snakes, Ander replied.

Bugs? Could Rod be desperate enough to eat bugs? He must be miserable and sick. He must be starving. She started to cry.

Krissy heard Ander's comments and she, too, started to sob. *I've done it again, I've made things worse for Krissy by getting upset.*

"Come on, Krissy," Jane said. "You don't really think your dad is eating bugs, do you? Of course he's not. TV is make-believe. Don't believe everything you see."

Krissy seemed to buy her explanation, and Jane felt better after convincing her. She found that if she said something often enough, she started to believe it herself.

Ander's release also brought with it a stunning development for the families back in Edmonton—the brief letters the guerrillas allowed the hostages to write. A couple of days after Ander's press conference in Quito, Jane received a faxed copy of Rod's note. She shook with excitement when she saw his handwriting. It was Rod's scrawl, no doubt about it.

"To Jane and Krissy, Love you very much and miss you very much. We are all OK. We are waiting to come home soon. Love Rod Dunbar."

He really is still alive. They've released one hostage and once they get what they want, they'll release Rod too.

By the next day, however, Jane's ebullient mood had evaporated. It was as if an irreversible pattern had developed—every time she took a step forward, she was blindsided and took three back.

The letter means nothing. All it means is he was alive a couple of weeks ago. By now he could be dead. They all could be.

Night Marches

ANDER'S PREDICTION THAT his fellow ecotourists would not be held long proved prophetic. On October 4, Day 24 of the kidnapping, the guerrillas gathered the captives together and announced that Sabine, Jesus and Maria would be released.

Rod was surprised, not that the trio was being let go, but that the event was so emotional. It was a bittersweet day for Rod; he envied Sabine and the honeymooning Spaniards their impending freedom, but he also knew they, like Ander, would never have been taken if he and the other United workers hadn't travelled to Ecuador to work on the pipeline.

Before Sabine, Jesus and Maria were released, the guerrillas allowed the pipeliners to write longer, more expansive letters to their families and friends. The same rules about content applied to these letters as to the first: no details about their whereabouts (as if they had a clue), no details about the kidnappers. The United workers were to urge their families to plead with the company to start negotiating for their release. "Company, company," the guerrillas said, pounding their fists into their hands. "Pressure. Pressure."

For most of the hostages, the second letters weren't as difficult to write as the first, but they were still hard. Rod, especially, wanted to make the most of this opportunity to contact his family after recovering from his horrible illness, but he found it tricky to convey everything he wanted to say.

Rod wrote:

Dear Jane and Krissy,

If you get this letter, it means I'm still here and OK. I miss you guys a lot and can't wait to get home. We will be on a long holiday when I get there. Hope Krissy is doing OK in school. I know she is. Can't talk about what is going on here and don't want to. Say hi to everybody back home and see them all soon. I spend the days thinking about the work to do to the house and yard when I get there. Miss you guys a lot. Love you all. See you soon.

Love, Rod.

Sabine, Jesus and Maria left the camp with the letters and with hugs from the remaining hostages. Rod teased Barney as he traded watches with Jesus; the Canadian had a self-illuminating Timex Indiglo purchased at a Wal-Mart in Edmonton, the Spaniard had a designer Heineken watch from Europe. Rod thought Barney ended up with a raw deal, but Barney insisted the Heineken watch was cooler.

"Well, how are you going to see your watch now at night, Barnz?" Rod said. Barney grinned. He hadn't thought of that.

Part of Rod guiltily wished that Jesus and Maria could stay because it would make the pipeliners' time in the jungle more tolerable. He would miss Maria, the tiny dynamo who'd stuck up for him when he was so sick. Maria wasn't shy about sharing information with the pipeliners, either. She confided in Rod that she, Jesus and Sabine were told to give misleading details to authorities about the hostages' whereabouts, that they'd marched through vast cocaine fields, and crossed a large river—presumably the San Miguel, which separates Colombia and Ecuador north of Lago Agrio—in a ferry boat. It was obvious the guerrillas wanted to trick the Ecuadorean army into believing they were in Colombia, but Maria hadn't yet decided if she would co-operate. She told Rod she was worried about the consequences of each of her choices.

Before their goodbyes, the trio gave the United workers much of the gear they'd taken from their van when they were captured—fly nets, a first-aid kit, blankets. After the goodbyes, the pipeliners were led one way by the main guerrilla group, and Sabine and the Spaniards were taken in the opposite direction by a small splinter group. Rod watched them trudge off.

Good luck. Don't forget about us in here.

From the start, Barney was the hostages' resident pessimist, miring the other men in the mud of his gruesome dreams and the muck of his despairing sullenness. It was a 180-degree change from his pre-ordeal personality—sunny, fun-loving, congenial—but he couldn't snap out of it. Everything his uncle had warned him about kidnapping in South America was coming true. He worried constantly that he might die in the jungle.

His physical state was better. Despite his asthma, he was still strong as a bull and handled the forced night marches and grotesque food as well as any of the men.

But even Barney was pushed to his limits during a particularly bizarre journey just days after Sabine, Maria and Jesus were released.

The hike started around 6 p.m., just after sundown, with a call of "*Vamoose*" from one of the guerrilla scouts who led the group. The kidnappers, confident they were a comfortable distance from military searchers, led the march through the gummy mud on a roadside at the jungle's edge. As instructed, the hostages tried to follow in the kidnappers' and in each other's footsteps, to make it appear there was only one set of tracks.

Barney was heartened when the hostages received a rare bit of information about their destination: the guerrilla commander told them they were to meet a car further down the road in three hours. *Maybe we won't have to walk any more. Maybe we're being taken to a guarded building somewhere.*

It began to rain, a cold, hard drizzle, but even through the murky gloom Barney and the others spotted a farmer leading a donkey down the trail. The guerrillas immediately pushed the hostages into the bush, shoving them to the ground, hovering over them with guns drawn. The hostages watched the farmer pass and, from the shocked look on his face, it was clear they'd been seen. The alarmed farmer did not, however, stop to inquire why so many armed men happened to be in the bush standing guard over eight *gringos*. He whipped his donkey wildly and got the hell out of there.

Who can blame him? He's scared.

The guerrillas, leery from their close call, veered away from the road and led the hostages down a partly cleared trail through the jungle. Half-metre high stumps jutted up from the ground where the bush had been thinned with machetes. But the guerrillas' flashlights illuminated the path only rarely, and Barney stumbled through the snotty mixture of mud and animal manure. Rain-saturated leaves swatted him as he passed.

Suddenly, Barney's ankle twisted violently as his foot slid into a gaping rut in the trail. *Just like a horse going into a gopher hole in Alberta,* he thought wildly. Barney fell into the mud, slapping his hands over his mouth to stifle a scream. After a few seconds, he tried to stand but immediately splashed back down into the mud. Frantic that he might be left behind, despite the excruciating pain, he began crawling on his hands and knees through the muck and cowshit, dodging tree stumps, trying desperately to keep up with the pack. He was covered with mud and manure; he tasted their bitterness in his mouth.

If I don't keep up, they'll either abandon me or shoot me and say I tried to escape. I gotta keep going.

Word travelled quickly up the line that something had happened to Barney. Rod, at the front of the pack, stumbled his way back through the mud and stumps to Barney, who was lying flat on his back, his face straining with the agony and exhaustion.

Barney grimaced as Rod eased off his boot to survey the damage. The problem was apparent at once—Barney's ankle was already swollen to the size of a softball.

"Fuck, he broke it! It's probably a fucking compound fracture!" Rod said, directing his anger to no one in particular. "Does this march have to be done tonight? We can't see and now his leg is broken!"

One of the guerrillas pushed Rod aside, stooped over Barney and jammed a rag into his mouth to muffle his cries. He poured alcohol over Barney's foot, which was shredded with insect bites, open sores and blisters worn raw by the inside of his wet leather boot. Barney suppressed another scream as the alcohol seared his flesh, and yet another when the guerrilla grabbed his ankle and twisted it back and forth.

To Barney's amazement, the kidnapper somehow was able to massage the swelling away from the injury and up his leg. The guerrilla wrapped the ankle in a bandana and placed Barney's boot back on.

Still, Barney worried that the guerrilla's handiwork, however ingenious, wouldn't be enough to allow him to keep marching. Mindful of the car they were supposed to meet in a couple of hours, he asked Rod and Colin to help him. They didn't hesitate. They picked him up and carried him fireman-style a few steps down the trail through the ankle-deep ooze. But Colin, who had chronic knee problems, felt his kneecap give. Rod's hip twinged. The three of them fell, Barney flat on his ass.

"This is crazy. It's not going to work," said Barney.

Barney motioned to one of the guerrillas, using a series of hand gestures to ask if he could use his machete to cut a walking stick from a tree limb. The kidnapper agreed and cut a stick for Barney, who attempted in this way to make it on his own.

Where the trail was wide enough, Colin and Rod walked on either side of Barney, helping to support his weight. Where the trail was narrow or climbed a hill, Barney crawled on all fours.

On one section of the trail, Barney started to crawl across a fallen log. He put his hand on the top of its stump but whipped it back and started screaming. One of the guerrillas shone his flashlight on the log—dozens of enormous ants the size of Barney's pinky finger covered the stump. Three had stung Barney's hand, which was already swelling. *Congos! I'm a dead man!* Fortunately, the venom proved not to be immediately fatal, although Barney had to wrap his throbbing hand in a rag so he could hold on to his walking stick.

Now, with two of his four limbs badly damaged, Barney still forged ahead. But soon all the captives were too exhausted to move another step. The guerrilla leader motioned to his watch. "*Caro,*" he said. We have to make the car.

The prospect of sitting in an automobile galvanized the captives, as did a rare reinforcement of cigarettes from the guerrillas. They trudged on for another hour-and-a-half until, finally, they saw the car, a battered AMC Eagle four-wheel-drive with blown-out windows.

The guerrillas didn't pause to admire the automobile. A kidnapper pushed Barney and Colin towards the car. It seemed they were being split off from the main group, but Barney was in no position to protest. His head was pushed down by the kidnappers so that he couldn't catch a glimpse of the driver. *Why would I want to see the driver?* Colin fell in beside him, and the two were quickly blindfolded with smelly rags as the driver gunned the motor. *Either they're taking me underground to get medical attention or they're going to shoot me and dump my body beside the road because I'm a nuisance to them.*

Inexplicably, the driver travelled down the bumpy road for only a few minutes. Then Barney and Colin, still blindfolded, were hauled from the car and pushed into the back of what seemed to be a cattle truck covered in a tarp. There they huddled for several minutes, protected from the rain but bewildered about what would come next. Barney tried to ask Colin what was happening, but was quickly silenced by a guerrilla's sharp "Shh!"

About fifteen minutes later, Barney heard the scrapes and bumps of more people climbing into the back of the truck, but he was still blindfolded and couldn't see who they were. Since the rainy gloom was so dark, the new arrivals apparently had the same problem, and Barney soon heard someone whisper: "Who is that?"

"It's Barney. Rod? Is that you?"

"Yeah," said Rod. "What's going on? Where are we going?"

"I have no idea. I hoped you would know."

More guerrillas jumped into the back of the truck, one ripped both their blindfolds away, and then the vehicle was off, lurching down the muddy road. But it wasn't long before its bald tires bogged down in the mire. It was stuck.

But the guerrillas, seemingly prepared for any logistical problem, had a back-up plan: The rundown AMC Eagle, which had been following the truck, transported the hostages and guerrillas three and four at a time through a nearby village and onto a major highway. The speed they were now moving was dizzying to Barney, who'd been used to moving at a slug's pace through the bush on his ruined ankle.

One after the other, the groups of hostages were dumped by the roadside, then hustled up a hill. In the hour it took for everybody to arrive at the hill's summit, the night skies opened up and began to pour.

Barney, fatigued and soaked, fell asleep, hoping that the guerrillas would take pity on the hostages and stop the march. But the kidnappers were not close to being finished. The jungle terrain was even rougher than before—high hills, pockmarked with deep swamps, carved by fast-flowing creeks. Still, the guerrillas insisted the group keep moving on. Barney's ankle throbbed with every step and he grew more and more frustrated at being kept clueless about their final stopping-place or how long they were expected to keep up this pace. Vengeful thoughts filled his mind, but he had no target on which to expel his wrath, and his fury just drained him even more.

Just past midnight, the guerrillas stopped the group. *Finally. Thank God. We're finally done.* Barney huddled together with the other hostages for warmth under the trees, preparing to sleep. But soon their unsympathetic captors roused them yet again, forcing them to march on for several more hours.

Still pitch black, it was so cold that Barney could see his breath. He actually thought hypothermia could become a danger, an enormous irony considering how warm it became during the day. To make matters worse, Barney slipped several times into the fast-flowing streams and swamps that criss-crossed their route. Twice he fell into swamps so deep he couldn't touch bottom and frantically he dog-paddled to the other side. Even the normally sure-footed guerrillas fell, slipping on the slimy logs that crossed the water.

And then, at last, after nearly twelve hours, it was over. The guerrillas stopped the group beside a deep, churning river, as wide as a city street. They attached a hammock to two tree trunks and allowed Barney to lie there to rest his leg. The other hostages paired off, stripped to the waist, huddled back-to-back under damp blankets, sharing what little body heat they had left.

As he tried to make himself comfortable in the wet and the cold, Barney silently cursed the guerrillas for making him walk on his destroyed ankle. *One day I'll make them pay for this.*

After their epic night march, the guerrillas cut the pace slightly, but for several days they continued to force the hostages onward. For some reason, the guerrillas outfitted Barney in full camouflage gear and had him carry an unloaded machine gun on all the hikes. He now looked like one of the kidnappers and Rod teased him, but Barney found no humour in his jokes. He worried that if the guerrillas ever did face off with the army, he'd be thrust into the open as a decoy to be cut down by the soldiers' gunfire while the guerrillas made their escape. It was the only explanation he could come up with.

Finally, the guerrillas and the hostages reached an encampment. Whether it was food poisoning, stress over fearing that the army would shoot him, or the after-effects of their exhausting marches, Barney became afflicted at the camp with what at first appeared to be same sickness Rod had barely managed to fight off. But, as the illness continued to rage, it soon became clear that Barney had it much, much worse.

For eight days he lay stiff in his hammock, feverish with gut-churning diarrhea and continuous dry heaves. Everything he ate or drank, he immediately vomited up, including a veritable pharmacy of anti-malaria and anti-cholera pills fed to him by the guerrillas. In an isolated moment of non-delirium, Barney joked to the other men that he felt like a Pez dispenser. The pills left him as quickly as the guerrillas could jam them in.

Several nights in a row, as he drifted into a light, feverish sleep, Barney panicked, worried he wouldn't wake up again. His asthma was bad, and he was down to using the inhaler fetched for him by the guerrillas that was only one-quarter his regular inhaler's strength. He coughed and wheezed; his lungs were full of liquid.

In a desperate haze, he told Barry to pass along a message to his family. He wanted them to know that he had fought the illness but could not win.

"Tell them I tried," he told Barry. "Tell them I did my best."

One morning, Barney's fever seemed to have reached its zenith. He could feel the heat rolling off himself in waves. If he'd the luxury of a mirror, and the energy to look into it, he would have seen a stranger peering back at him, a hollow-cheeked nightmare with cloudy, blood-red eyes. He knew he smelled terrible, lying as he was in a hammock stained with vomit, feces and sweat.

"We've got to get your ass down to the creek to cool you down and blow the stink off you," Rod told him. Too weak to refuse, he let himself be dragged from his cloth bunk, clad only in under-

wear and a T-shirt, his ankle still swollen and sore, and steered towards the water.

Barney stumbled and nearly fell on the path to the water several times, once precariously close to some sharp, jutting rocks, but he managed to make it. As he sat naked in the creek's frigid current, he thought that his feverish body would bring the water to a boil. Rod splashed his face with water and Barney felt his heart nearly stop; he drew in a sharp breath and his eyes rolled back in his head.

"Jesus, he's going to pass out!" Rod exclaimed.

But after a few minutes, Barney started to feel a bit better, a bit rejuvenated. He remained in the stream for several more minutes, slack-limbed and goose-bumped, until he felt able to stand and lurch his way back to his hammock under his own power.

Once back in his hammock under the tarpaulin shelter, after Rod's persistent advice, he vowed to stop taking the guerrilla's pills. Rod convinced him they were making him sicker. From now on, Barney would accept only aspirin and reject the multi-hued horse pills the kidnappers tried to force-feed him.

The next day, Barney was well enough to carry his hammock and blanket down to the creek to wash them. Over the next few days his strength slowly returned, and he was able to put more and more weight on his ankle. Gradually, his diarrhea disappeared and Barney was almost relieved to be constipated again.

When he'd finally rid his body of the mysterious illness, Barney took Rod aside. He thanked his friend for saving his life, both on the night walk when he had nearly snapped his ankle and at the height of his fever. He told Rod he could never have made it without his friend's help. Rod told Barney that's what friends did.

They sat together in silence, looking at their sad little shelter, the filthy clothes hanging from the tree-trunk supports and watched the guerrillas pace about like panthers around the encampment. The clouds were low—it was about to pour again—and the atmosphere was as gloomy and grey as a funeral parlour's.

Barney sighed, his lungs giving a residual little rattle.

"I can't wait to get out of here, man," he sighed, a despondent note in his voice. "I want to go home so bad."

"I hear you, Barnz," Rod said, but in an optimistic frame of mind, added, "We can see the light at the end of the tunnel now, buddy. It's near."

Barney brightened a bit; Rod had a knack for telling him exactly what he needed to hear.

"It would have been shitty if I'd died just a few days before we were released, eh?" Barney said.

"Yeah, it would have been."

Rod slapped Barney on the back and the two old friends shook their heads and laughed.

———

On October 8, just before midnight, while Barney was becoming frighteningly ill at the encampment deep in the jungle, Sabine, Jesus and Maria were discovered by a farmer near Tarapoa, who guided them to a military patrol. Word of their release travelled quickly. The Allied Intelligence reps, through their contacts in Sucumbios province, heard the news and telephoned Sgt. Gord Black in Quito.

At 1:30 a.m. on October 9, Gord was finally asleep in his hotel room, exhausted after a string of twenty-hour days spent preparing for the difficult nightly negotiations with the guerrillas, who'd knocked their ransom demand down only slightly to $15 million. The Allied people told Gord they believed Sabine and the Spaniards were being guarded by the military at The Block, City Investing's compound, and that they were trying to arrange medical help and transport back to Quito for the released hostages. Gord told them he'd be there as soon as he could to accompany Sabine.

Because planes could not land at The Block's airstrip in the dark—it possessed only a crude, low-tech beacon to guide landing planes—Gord left at dawn, with Ambassador Kneale and Danielle Beaudoin, a fellow Canadian who worked with Sabine at the radio station ALER. Gord brought along Beaudoin so Sabine would see a familiar, friendly face.

Midway through the flight, as the airplane crossed the cordillera and flew over the first verdant patches of the Oriente jungle, Gord, who was also a pilot, realized how difficult landing at The Block's strip would be. Gord could see from the craft's tiny window that the clouds were beginning to form inordinately low, almost hugging the ground. A landing on The Block's strip would be nearly impossible in these conditions.

As the plane descended, Gord became terrified that he and the other passengers' lives were in real danger. The pilots had come out of the clouds too far down the runway to allow for a safe landing. Immediately, they went into what is called a missed approach, pitched the plane nose-up at full power and threw it straight into the sky. Gord shook his head in disbelief. No pilot in his right mind would have dared to land under these conditions.

The pilots landed instead at Lago Agrio where Gord, Kneale and Beaudoin met a representative from City Investing. Quito's climate was wonderful, like Vancouver's on a rare sunny late-spring day, but Lago Agrio's humid, sweltering stench surprised them.

Their intention was to wait at Lago Agrio until the weather at Tarapoa cleared. But Gord's curiosity was aroused when he entered the airport to find dozens of Ecuadorean soldiers milling about. He'd expected to see some sort of military presence—the search effort for the hostages was still in full-swing just a few kilometres away—but the sheer numbers of soldiers at the airport led him to believe something was up.

His suspicions were soon confirmed when a young Ecuadorean soldier approached. Gord was certainly not wearing the RCMP's traditional red serge, but because he was white, over six feet tall and about 200 pounds, he looked North American. The private assumed he and Kneale were in Lago Agrio because of the freed hostages and said he had some information he'd be interested in trading, *quid pro quo*.

Gord took the thinly veiled hint and shuffled through his bag, producing a remarkable first-aid kit he'd brought from Ottawa. It contained every imaginable variety of jungle antidote, even a complete minor-surgery kit. The young soldier's eyes lit up, then widened even more when the City Investing representative offered him a plane ticket to Quito, which would spare the army man the ten-hour drive. The soldier confided that Sabine and the Spaniards were, in fact, being held here in Lago Agrio ever since they encountered the military patrol shortly after midnight.

Gord immediately called his superiors in Ottawa to apprise them of the changed situation. Ambassador Kneale dialed one of Ecuador's top-ranking generals, demanding to know where Sabine was. An hour-and-a-half later, two Ecuadorean army colonels met the Canadian delegation at the airport. Kneale was forthright in his demands. "She's a Canadian. I want her and I want her now," he told the colonels. "We need to get these people looked after medically."

The colonels said they'd check into it and an hour later, a military convoy appeared at the airport. Sabine emerged from one of the vehicles, looking gaunt, dirty and weary.

Across the tarmac, Sabine spotted Gord, and headed straight for him.

Before Gord could take a step, an Ecuadorean soldier stepped toward him and shoved an M-16 barrel into his stomach. Gord looked first at the gun in his abdomen and then at the soldier, who was staring at him. Gord stared right back.

Is this guy going to shoot me here in the middle of the jungle with my ambassador watching? Gord imagined what the soldier was thinking: "This is my country, I don't know why you're here or what you think you're doing," but he didn't care. He grabbed the gun by its barrel and shoved it away, not once averting his gaze.

After a pregnant pause, the soldier backed off and Gord grabbed Sabine and hustled her into a room already stocked by Allied Intelligence with medical kits and staffed by a local doctor. Jesus and Maria followed close behind. Once safely inside, Gord handed Sabine his cell phone and said, "Call your family." She did, while waiting to be examined, and spoke to her parents.

"I'm OK. I'm free," she told them, crying. "No, really, it's true." She told them she had an RCMP officer with her and Gord's heart soared. He looked around the room, and saw that nearly everyone had tears in their eyes—the doctor, the Allied man. Gord, himself, fought off a surge of emotion.

After a twenty-minute medical Sabine was cleared to go, but Gord knew they'd have to brave a phalanx of authorities before they reached the plane. "Hang on to my arm," Gord told Sabine. "Don't stop for any reason. Just hold tight." Though she was barely five-foot-five, her grip left indented marks on his arm.

They waded sixty metres through a throng of media and tense soldiers, Jesus and Maria close on their heels. Once they'd all boarded, the pilot fired up the engines and headed for Quito.

Well, that was interesting, Gord thought, exhaling deeply as the plane rose above the jungle canopy. *That's one Canadian down,* he thought. *Only seven to go.*

In Quito, Sabine, Jesus and Maria met with police and military officials, who quizzed them about the guerrillas. Their arrival in the capital was cheered by members of ALER, Sabine and Ander Mimenza's educational radio project. The station's walls were by now papered with letters of encouragement from non-profit groups throughout the world. They extinguished the last three of the four candles they had lit after the capture, tiny flames that represented the lives of Ander, Sabine, Jesus and Maria.

After tearful farewells to ALER station workers and final briefings with diplomatic and military officials, Jesus and Maria flew home to Bilbao, Spain, and Sabine to Montreal.

Back in Canada, Sabine spoke to reporters about her captors' tenacity and lack of fear.

"They were not scared of the military," she said. The kidnappers "killed (Edison Jacome) on the first day, so I think they are prepared to kill people."

She also reported, just as the guerrillas had ordered, that she thought the hostages were being held across the border in Colombia, in direct contradiction to the Ecuadorean officials, who insisted they were still in Ecuador. In fact, in the days following their release, Ecuadorean army leaders said they'd learned nothing new from Sabine, Jesus and Maria and even suggested that they were withholding information or propagating the Colombia story to prevent the United workers from getting caught in a confrontation between the military and the guerrillas.

The army's search operation continued, but fruitlessly. Wherever it was the guerrillas were leading the pipeliners on their night marches, it was working.

Mr. and Mrs. Tiger Tooth

FOR THE PAST MONTH, from the moment the hostages were captured, the guerrillas guarded them with stoicism, military exactness and the ever-present threat of immediate violence. They cleaned their weapons nightly in front of the hostages, sometimes with the barrels levelled directly at the hostages' heads, a situation Rod found to be overwhelmingly nervewracking. The abductors had rarely spoken to him and the other pipeliners, relying instead on Sabine or the Spaniards to translate their orders. By now Rod was utterly disoriented after dozens of forced marches that criss-crossed the jungle. He had no idea where his next scant meal or cigarette was coming from, let alone how negotiations with United Pipeline were going. But he was not about to hound his captors for information, not when the guerrillas sat grim-faced and menacing, their thumbs idly clicking the safeties on their M-16s.

In early October, however, after Sabine and the Spaniards were released, the guerrillas loosened up a little. They became less persistent in following the hostages into the jungle during bathroom breaks. The knew the hostages would consider the option of escaping and hacking their way through the malarial jungle too daunting. And now that Sabine, Maria and Jesus were freed, the kidnappers were forced to communicate with the hostages through a dog's breakfast of Spanish and butchered English.

The United workers, to a degree, also relaxed. Although none of the kidnappers had discussed the ransom yet, two things were clear: They were being held for a sizable sum of cash, and they were worth much more to their captors alive and in good health than dead and hacked to pieces in the dense jungle undergrowth. The fifteen guerrillas still waved around a frightening arsenal of weapons, but with not quite the same glowering intensity they had in the past.

Rod, who knew the most Spanish among the Canadians—which wasn't saying much—was elected the group's spokesperson. Since Barry's authority had been completely erased by the pipeliners, Rod became the hostages' *de facto* leader.

Still, he had second thoughts about accepting this responsibility. He was reluctant to be seen as the leader, as a guy the guerrillas would put holes in to illustrate the consequences of a false move. *If the kidnappers think we're getting too organized, maybe they'll take me out to the road and put a plug in my head to demonstrate exactly who is in control.*

Still, we're starving and sick. We've got no information. We can't be hurt any worse. What the hell? I'll do it.

Rod began keeping a list of Spanish words and phrases with their English translations on a dog-eared piece of paper. The smothering humidity smudged the list's ink, but he still managed to refer to it to string the odd sentence together.

As he and the others talked to the guerrillas, the kidnappers' personalities started to emerge.

The guerrillas all appeared deeply religious, not to mention vain. Many carried tiny mirrors adorned with pictures of Christ and the Virgin Mary on the back and wore gold crosses hung on necklaces. Although they all spoke Spanish, they seemed to have different accents as if, perhaps, they were from different countries. Rod compared the speech variances to the way a Montrealer and Parisian would speak French with different intonation and slang. He developed his own theory about the identity of the kidnappers—the leaders were former members of one of Colombia's revolutionary groups and the rest were common, if high-aiming, bandits brought together for the job from all over the continent's northwest corner.

There seemed to be two distinct camps in the gangster group—a handful of older, more experienced guerrillas and an equal number of younger rookies learning the ins and outs of the kidnapping game from the old pros.

Since the guerrillas did not reveal their given names, the hostages assigned nicknames to each one.

Commandant, the tall, sturdy, forty-ish commander of the group, carried himself with a quiet, regal air, like a camouflaged South American dictator. His subordinates treated him as such, hustling to grab him coffee from the portable stove, hanging onto his every word. Perhaps he was a disgruntled former Ecuadorean army commander, or a former Colombian revolutionary who'd broken away to start his own hostage-taking business. Whatever the case, when he said jump, his men never asked why. He ruled with absolute authority, treating the hostages with professional detachment. He often left the camp for extended periods; the other guerrillas would communicate with him during his absence using a lunchpail-size army-type radio with a long, drooping antenna.

Second-in-command was Joto, a fitter younger man whom the hostages pegged as Commandant's son. The two were close and often huddled in what seemed like familial conversation.

Muscles—probably, like Commandant, in his forties—was so dubbed because of his astonishing physique. He paraded around the camp without a T-shirt, displaying his washboard stomach, as if the jungle floor were the stage for a Mr. Ecuador bodybuilding contest. Sometimes the guerrillas play-wrestled or joked around by pointing their guns at one another. No one, however, screwed with Muscles. If the Commandant was the kidnappers' decision-maker and ruler, Muscles was their undisputed physical leader.

On marches he would bring up the rear, coiled and ready to tear up encroaching army soldiers with his M-16 or his bare hands for that matter. He had little contact with the hostages, preferring to terrify them by grimacing and pointing his gun at them.

Muscles' older brother was Big Mac, who was named after a particularly appalling meal from the hands of Chemaisu, an acne-scarred guerrilla who professed a love for English heavy metal groups like Black Sabbath and Iron Maiden and often cooked for the entire camp. One evening, as both the guerrillas and hostages choked down supper—a thin gruel of rice, oddly muddy broth and gristly boiled chicken—Big Mac walked past the Canadians. He looked forlornly at the food, shook his head at the United workers and said, with equal parts longing and hunger, "Big Mac." It was one of the few English phrases he knew.

Another similarly aged kidnapper was Lario, the clumsy guerrilla who lost one of his contact lenses in the jungle and who'd broken up Neil and Colin's fight. When Barney had needed a refill of his asthma inhaler, it was Lario who arranged for one to be fetched. He tried to sneak the hostages extra smokes and oatmeal. Of all the guerrillas, Lario seemed to sympathize most with the pipeliners' plight. Rod hated all the guerrillas with a passion, but he at least felt reasonably comfortable with Lario.

Lario, who said he used to be a teacher, tried to teach Rod Spanish, and Rod reciprocated with basic English lessons. The bespectacled guerrilla talked often about his son, a teenager who took business classes at university. In fact, many of the guerrillas spoke fondly of their families and hoped to be home for Christmas. The kidnappers stole or discarded most of the Canadians' personal effects, but they didn't take from the hostages anything their wives or families had given them. One of the guerrillas, early in the kidnapping, asked Rod for his gold chain, which Jane had bought him for their wedding. But Rod said, "No, *esposa*"—spouse in English—and the kidnapper backed off.

The oldest guerrillas were Old Tracker, a wizened, grey-haired trail scout in his late fifties who led marches with a compass and a Bushnell 10X rifle scope in his hands, and Luki, a heavy-set man who once proclaimed his love both for his wife and for salsa dancing. Some nights, Commandant allowed his men to turn on a small black transistor radio the size of a man's wallet. The weak signal from either a nearby Ecuadorean village or from across the border in Colombia would waft through the camp, playing some bouncy South American tune. Luki would put one hand on his stomach, extend the other and cut a Latin rug in front of his tent. In broken English, he told the hostages he could not wait to trade his rubber boots for black dancing shoes and take his wife to a club. Luki also fancied himself a sharpshooter, often bragging he could take down an army helicopter with a few precise bursts from his machine gun.

The younger group included Michael, a handsome, dark-eyed young guerrilla in his late teens, and Goldstar, who wore what appeared to be an Ecuadorean army star on his hat. Goldstar seemed superstitious about the medal, and wouldn't let anyone else touch it. There was also Vladimir, an apprentice scout in his late twenties also known as Young Tracker, and Fabio, a pudgy teenager who amused everybody with magic rope tricks. But Fabio had his deadly side, too. He was a bomb expert, and would show Rod which ground-hugging plants were best for concealing explosives. He also boasted about how many men he'd killed, and grinned malevolently while describing how he cut the ears from his victims and pinned them to a tree.

Rod asked Fabio if he'd learned his trade in the army. "No, no," Fabio said. "Guerrilla. *Cinco años*. Five years." Fabio told Rod he had a girlfriend who was also a guerrilla and was away on another job. "You better hope she's not getting poked by the other guerrillas, Fabio," Rod said. Fabio said his girlfriend wouldn't do that to him.

One guerrilla, an inscrutable, hulking man with aboriginal features, was known only as "the big Indian." He was as unreadable and frightening as Muscles.

Perhaps the most unlikely kidnappers were Mr. Tiger Tooth, a forty-ish scout, and his pretty, raven-haired teenaged bride. Both Mr. and Mrs. Tiger Tooth wore tiger incisors on gold chains around their necks, next to what appeared to be wedding rings. Mr. Tiger Tooth, judging from the slashes and raised scars on his hands, looked like he'd removed the teeth himself from a live, uncaged cat.

Mr. and Mrs. Tiger Tooth

Mr. and Mrs. Tiger Tooth shared a hammock and often kissed. He would point to her stomach and rub it, leading Rod to believe she was pregnant. They were quite obviously in love. On marches, though, the pair was all business. Mr. Tiger Tooth would take turns leading the entourage with Old Tracker, and Mrs. Tiger Tooth, hauling a huge pack that outweighed her by at least forty pounds, would pair up with a guerrilla in the middle of the line, brandishing an M-16 and a gleaming automatic Beretta pistol, which she dismantled and cleaned with startling efficiency every day.

The two were inseparable until Mrs. Tiger Tooth was attacked by a venomous snake during one of the camps the guerrillas made after Maria, Jesus and Sabine were released. Rod did not see the attack, but he heard the young woman's screams, and guessed what had happened when guerrillas swarmed the trees with machetes, shredding the trees and seeking out the poisonous serpent. Although the guerrillas carried antidotes to combat the worst the jungle's creatures could dish out, Rod heard Mrs. Tiger Tooth vomiting that night outside her tent and wondered if she had miscarried. In the morning, she was led away from the camp and disappeared.

The next morning, Rod asked Lario what had happened, but Lario would not reply.

By mid-October, the hostages, who were now more brazen with their captors, agreed that Rod should ask how much the kidnappers were seeking from United Pipeline. Commandant replied as though he'd been expecting the question. He said the company, and the North American oil industry in general, had to pay dearly for the environmental and economic damage it had done to Ecuador. "Fifteen million, U.S.," he said.

Rod was stunned. There was no way United, a small company headquartered in Durango, Colorado with a small branch office in Edmonton, could drum up fifteen million in cash. Before approaching Commandant, the hostages had guessed at the amount they might fetch. The consensus was a bit over a hundred grand for each of the eight workers—maybe a million American dollars in total. But fifteen million? That was insanity.

As for the guerrillas' assertion that Canadian companies had to pay for the environmental and economic problems they'd created in Ecuador, Rod thought that was just a bullshit cop-out, a way for the guerrillas to rationalize their greed. City Investing always hired locals, at better-than-average salaries, to complement foreign crews. And environmental standards were much more rigorously upheld by the Canadian oil companies than the Ecuadorean outfits. When it drilled for crude oil, City Investing captured the salty, corrosive underground water that came out of the ground with the petroleum and pumped it several thousand metres back into the earth. Ecuadorean oil companies pumped the saltwater straight into the rain forest, where it caused damage to the lush ecosystem.

Rod walked up to Commandant, shook his hand, and said, "I guess we're going to become close friends. If you want fifteen million, we're going to be together for a long time." Commandant, who did not suffer sarcasm gladly, scowled at him. Rod thought he might pay for being cheeky to the commander, but he was so dismayed by the inflated ransom amount that he didn't care.

That night, the hostages discussed the ransom demand.

"It's crazy. Fifteen million U.S. is like 22 million Canadian," Rod said. "The company is not going to pay 22 million to get eight of us out of here."

But Colin was optimistic the company would send negotiators to Ecuador to whittle the figure down. "They'll negotiate and United will pay the ransom to get us out of here," Colin said. "I'm sure my wife is in there every day kicking (United general manager) Ken Foster's ass. And my Dad is probably in there every day, pressuring the company. 'Let's get this done. Let's get them out of there.'"

But Barney didn't buy any of it.. "They're going to boot-fuck us and kill us," he said of the guerrillas. "We're dead either way."

The next two weeks were a blur of days spent huddled under the tarpaulin and nights of endurance-testing marches. It rained three or four times a day, sometimes in torrents that snapped twenty-five-metre-high trees like dry twigs. During the day, the guerrillas set up camp on hillsides so they'd have a better vantage point in case the army discovered them. It was easier to shoot downhill than up, the guerrillas explained. But the strategy had its logistical disadvantages: rainwater flooded down the hill, soaking the pipeliners from head to toe.

At least the guerrillas were becoming more generous with supplies. Sometimes, two or three of the kidnappers would change into civilian clothes and run to a nearby village, or would arrange for locals to bring goods to them. One night two stocky farmers clad only in shorts sped by the hostages carrying sacks full of gear—ropes and cloth for more hammocks, food, rubber boots, soap, toilet paper. The locals left the supplies at the guerrillas' next planned encampment, and presumably were paid for their efforts, and for their silence. The men were delighted finally to have some soap to scrub the layers of dirt from their skin.

Once the supplies were in camp, Lario or one of the other kidnappers would duck under the hostages' tarpaulin with a bag full of goodies—baby powder, blankets, bowls, spoons, toothbrushes—and throw it on Rod's hammock. Rod would then distribute everything, being careful to keep the most tarnished spoons and the rattiest blankets for himself. It was a raw deal, but he didn't feel like fighting accusations he was hoarding the best gear.

The United workers were overjoyed the day they received more clothes, albeit cheap ones. Each man got a T-shirt, bikini briefs, nylon socks and nylon sweatpants, all with athletic apparel company logos on them. The pants were obviously knock-offs—the Nike swoosh was sideways and the Adidas symbol was in the middle of the knee. The clothes were poorly made, but at least they were something dry to change into. The guerrillas gave them rubber boots, too, which were much better in the rain than their leather workboots.

When it wasn't raining, the sun beat down through the jungle canopy from mid-morning to suppertime. The men spent hours in the stifling heat picking at ticks burrowed beneath their skin, pulling razor-sharp spikes out of their scalps.

Barney scratched at his crotch rot until it bled and scabbed over. Then he picked off the scabs. When he showed the scar tissue to Rod, Rod recoiled in horror.

The increasingly desperate situation made Rod ache for home more than ever. Rod vowed he'd never complain about an Alberta summer snowstorm or winter cold snap again.

To ease their misery, the men talked about life back in Canada. They were all roughnecks with roughneck hobbies—overhauling engines, re-painting Ski-Doo frames. They discussed the merits of the carburation system on the latest Harley Davidson Super-Glide model. Colin longed to get back to his acreage outside Edmonton to cut red cedar on his homemade mill. He and Barney scratched rough blueprints in the dirt for a new deck for Barney's house.

Rod, Barney and Grant hatched plans for leaving the pipeline game behind and opening a liquor store or pizza shop in Edmonton. Before becoming a pipeliner, Barney had worked in several pizza joints in the city and offered to teach the others the business. Neil would don a monkey suit and amuse customers as the restaurant's mascot.

And there were fleeting moments of bizarre levity that somehow made the captives' dispirited existence in the jungle more bearable.

Some of the guerrillas, behind the camouflage and intimidating facade, were complete characters. Michael and Goldstar, in addition to being criminals wanted throughout Ecuador, were unrepentant womanizers. The pair, both good-looking, rugged and dark-skinned, were often sent to nearby villages on supply missions. Invariably, they'd return to the camp at 4 a.m., drunker than Rod had ever been at his raunchiest.

One night, Michael and Goldstar, drenched in aftershave and reeking of booze, entered the hostages' shelter, awakened the hostages and pumped their hands, grinning ear-to-ear.

"Why are you so happy?" Rod asked Michael.

"*Dos chickilinas*," Michael boasted, holding up two fingers. He had been with two women at a whorehouse in town. Rod sleepily congratulated him on the feat, an impressive one in any hemisphere.

On one of their supply/sex missions, Michael and Goldstar brought back a chess board for the camp. The guerrillas all were expert players and allowed the hostages to play games among themselves. Leonard, who belonged to his high school's chess club in the U.S., was very good, as were Colin and Grant. Rod didn't know the game, but learned quickly, eventually winning more games than he lost. Barney complained that Rod showed no mercy when the two of them played.

"Well, Barnz, are you a man or a mouse? You're a girly chess player, aren't you?" Rod teased.

One afternoon, Rod walked across the encampment to the guerrillas' main tent. Most of them were inside, playing a few spirited games. Rod watched patiently, then challenged Commandant to a match. The lead guerrilla, an experienced, tactical player, tricked Rod into a checkmate within a minute. As the other guerrillas looked on laughing, Commandant made the now-familiar throat-slitting gesture, and placed a roll of toilet paper on Rod's head. The implication: Rod was a shithead.

Mr. and Mrs. Tiger Tooth

Rod had his revenge, though, when he reached a quick checkmate against Commandant in a rematch. After the game, Rod looked at Commandant and mimed a taunt. He pointed to his eye, his foot, then to the guerrilla leader and his own rear end. The implication: I kicked your ass. Commandant smiled and nodded.

Halloween came, and was significant for the hostages beyond the ghoulish nature of their situation: it was Barney's twenty-fourth birthday.

Barney knew the date because he kept track of the months and days in the jungle with an old trick he'd learned in grade school. He made fists and put them together side-by-side so the knuckles and backs of his hands pointed up. From right to left, he counted off the months: January was his pinky knuckle, February the hollow to the left of that, March the knuckle of his fourth finger, April the hollow left of that, and so on. The knuckles—January, March, May and July on his right hand; August, October and December on his left—were months with thirty-one days in them. The hollows—February, April and June on his right hand; September and November on his left—were months with thirty days, or in February's case, twenty-eight.

Barney told the guerrillas it was his birthday, and beseeched them for gifts. The kidnappers responded with tiny pieces of sour gum. From the hostages, Barney received one entire cigarette from their skimpy daily ration.

To Barney, a full cigarette—one that he didn't have to share with seven other guys—was like gold. But he didn't have the heart to smoke it all himself. "I gotta share my birthday cake with you guys," he said, passing the cigarette around to his friends.

That night, Barney woke up needing to go to the bathroom. *It's my birthday, I'm going out in my birthday suit.* He stepped from the tent and whistled for one of the guerrillas to come over with a flashlight—the standard procedure. The guard shone his light on Barney, but seeing the Canadian's substantial naked form, he fumbled the flashlight and quickly shut it off. Barney laughed and laughed. He felt better than he had since being taken.

Mr. and Mrs. Tiger Tooth

All things considered, it wasn't a bad birthday.

But the hostages' good humour did not last. Negotiations were dragging. Commandant told Rod they would be released on a certain day. But then the day would pass, and the Canadians' spirits would plunge.

The lack of food, cigarettes and medicine started to set the men off. Rod noticed it, but was too frustrated himself to try to rein anybody else in. He'd prided himself on staying level-headed and mentally strong in the jungle, but now he felt like a hypocrite, trying to convince Barnz and Grant and Skunk that things were OK. They weren't OK. They were terrible. Everybody was losing weight, and equal amounts of patience. Even Neil, who, apart from his fight with Colin, was an eternal optimist, snapped, shouting at the guerrillas: "Fifteen million! Fifteen million U.S. and you can't get us any tobacco?"

Rod pressured the guerrillas to do more to keep the hostages healthy. "Get us some medicine," he told Lario. "Our toenails are falling off, our feet are turning black. We've got crotch rot so bad we can't bend over because it cracks open and bleeds. You'll get lots of money for us if we're in good health. So get us some supplies!"

The night walks ceased—the guerrillas presumably thought the threat of being discovered by the Ecuadorean army had passed as they moved deeper into the jungle—but that did little to improve Rod's mood. They still often hiked during the day, and he was having an impossible time sleeping at night. He lay awake listening to the kidnappers' movements, tracking their locations, monitoring their shift changes. If he was lucky, he'd drift off around 4 or 5 a.m.

One morning in early November, just before daybreak, mere minutes after Rod had finally fallen asleep, Colin got up and started searching in the dark for his toothbrush. He kept what few supplies he had rolled up tightly in a thick plastic bag that rattled at the slightest touch.

Rod moaned: "Jesus, you guys. It's early. I'm trying to get some sleep here." Colin left the tent, brushed his teeth and came back to put his gear back in the bag, which rattled again.

"Colin," Rod growled. "Quit making that fucking noise or I'll stuff that bag down your goddamn throat!"

Colin, angry now as well, said, "What noise?" He walked over to Rod's hammock and crumpled the bag in Rod's face. "This noise?"

Blankets flew, Rod jumped up, nearly stepping on Skunk, who cowered in his hammock, and grabbed Colin by the shoulder and raised his right fist. "You son of a bitch, I could kill you right now."

Colin shrank away from the expected punch and said, in a small voice, "Jesus, Rod. Calm down, I didn't do it on purpose. I'm just brushing my teeth."

Rod said, "You son of a bitch. This is the closest to death you have ever come."

Rod looked at the other men under the shelter and saw the panic on their faces. *What am I doing? We can't fight each other. If we fight each other, we're just giving in to the guerrillas. If we fight each other, they win.* He calmed down before throwing the punch.

Still in his underwear, he walked out of the tent, put on his rubber boots, urinated, and sat on his haunches, watching the monkeys leap and squeal through the tops of the palms. He was so conflicted about how he was supposed to act in the jungle.

He wanted to be a rock, but the guerrillas were pounding him into dust.

Rod ducked back into the tent ten minutes later, shaking. "Sorry, man," he said to Colin. "I couldn't sleep again last night. I'd just fallen asleep when you woke me up."

"It's all right, Rod. We've just got to take it easy out here," said Colin.

"You're right, man," Rod said. "You're right."

But soon, more demoralizing news followed Colin's and Rod's scrap. In early November, the guerrillas told the hostages that United's bargaining team—Tio Conejo—had pulled the plug on negotiations. The guerrillas informed the hostages that they had told the negotiators they'd start "killing gringos" if they didn't get their $15 million. Word of the impasse enraged Barney, whose Halloween high had long since passed. He thought United had abandoned him and his buddies. *The only way out of this is to get a gun.*

Barney asked Old Tracker, with whom he got along reasonably well, to let him join the guerrillas. Old Tracker had boasted that the guerrilla group had blown up a pipeline belonging to Ecuador's nationalized petroleum company in the name of their anti-industry credo, spilling tens of thousands of barrels of oil. Barney said he wanted to join the cause. He made bomb and grenade launcher noises to demonstrate his sincerity. "Use me," Barney said. "I'm a *loco gringo.*"

But Old Tracker refused to give Barney a gun, perhaps suspecting the Canadian would turn his rage not on the North American oil industry, but on the guerrillas.

After failing to convince Old Tracker, Barney spiraled deeper into depression. Above all else he valued his freedom. But after his unsuccessful attempt he became inconsolable and his lurid, blood-soaked dreams resumed.

Rod was so near the breaking point himself he was unable to offer any comfort to Barney. Just days after Barney's plea to Old Tracker, Rod snapped. There was no particular incident that made him go off, just the compounded effects of lack of sleep, food and cigarettes. Rod was not a heavy smoker, perhaps three to six a day, but the jungle intensified his need for nicotine. When he needed a cigarette, he needed it *now*.

One sticky morning in early November, with the guerrillas out of earshot, he announced to the guys that he was going to bolt. Damn the snakes, damn the threat of disease, damn the fact that he didn't know how to get out of the jungle, he'd had enough.

"That's it, boys. I'm fucking out of here," he said to the group. "First chance I get, next time I'm on a trail and I got a machine gun in front of me and he's carrying a backpack, I'm pushing him to the ground, bashing in his head with a rock and taking that machine gun and I'm out of here."

The other hostages stared at him. "Don't do it, man," they said. "That's totally selfish. What's going to happen to us if you get killed?"

Neil said to Rod: "Think of your family."

Rod snapped back at him. "That's the problem, Neil. I am thinking of my family. I want to get home. I want to get out of here. Enough is enough. This is bullshit. What's the problem here? What is the value of a human life? If they're asking for $15 million, give it to them. If it's money they want, give it to them!"

But the hostages protested. "What about us?" one said. "They'll march a couple of us out on the road and kill us just to show if it happens again two more die. How will we know what happened to you if you get killed?"

Rod fumed, knotting his hands into tight fists. *Fuck you all. I'm sick of this. I'm gone. It's time to look out for number one.*

But he felt himself relax. He hung his head and began to realize his friends were right. *Even if I managed to grab a gun, I'd be able to kill maybe two of the guerrillas, three, tops. That still leaves a dozen. They'll hunt me down like a dog in the woods and skin me alive. They'll feed me to the snakes and scorpions just for entertainment. No matter how nice Lario tried to be, or Luki, they're all ruthless pricks who had put an arbitrary price on my life.*

And say I did get out. All the farmers around here are helping them. All of the locals are helping them. What if I go to one of their houses and see Muscles sitting there drinking coffee? He'll crush me like a bug.

Rod sighed and told the other guys he wouldn't run. Grant joked he was going to hide Rod's rubber boots so if he did try to escape, he'd have to do it in bare feet.

Still, the impulse to bolt remained with Rod, and he knew he wasn't the only one who felt that way.

Only a few days later, Neil devised his own escape plan. Sick of the stalled negotiations, Neil told the others the next time it rained, he was going to climb a enormous, fifty-metre-high tree behind the encampment and hide out there. He'd wedge himself between the tree's highest branches and survive on ants and leaves, until the guerrillas and the other pipeliners moved off to another camp. When the coast was clear, he'd scuttle back down the tree and flee through the jungle to civilization.

Rod knew Neil was an accomplished hunter and could probably pull it off, but he talked him out of it.

"Neil, just wait a couple of weeks and I'll be with you and we'll both make a good run at it," he said.

Neil thought it sounded like a plan. He walked off.

Colin approached Rod. "What were you guys talking about?" he asked.

"Nothing," Rod said, but that didn't fool Colin.

"Look," Colin said. "If you run, make sure you tell Karen and the kids I love them. Tell them I'll see them soon. Will you do that?"

Rod said he would.

Guerrilla Divide

THE GUERRILLAS WEREN'T stupid. Not only was their jungle acumen required to outwit the massive search effort undertaken by the Ecuadorean army, they had to be social scientists to recognize and manipulate their hostages' emotional valleys and plateaux. Though the guerrillas spoke little English, they sensed their hostages' mood swings from their body language and the tones of their voices. When they saw the hostages becoming restless and angry or scanning the bush, looking for the best place to attempt an escape, they placated them with extra cigarettes, or with a two-litre bottle of Coke. These were small gestures, but they kept the hostages from running.

The guerrillas were especially adept at controlling Barney, clearly the most depressed of the United workers, and consequently, the most likely to lash out. As early November brought with it chillier and more frequent rains, Barney became more despairing and sat through a particularly gloomy morning on November 11. Barney knew the date was Remembrance Day, and after observing a moment of silence at 11 a.m., he grew morose thinking about the grand ceremonies being held back in North America. He thought about the losses suffered by Canadian soldiers over the century, and reflected on how it so painfully mirrored his own loss in the jungle.

The guerrillas, sensing Barney's agony, brought the radio over to him, tuning it to a rural station. Barney wasn't in the mood for canned salsa music, but, to his shock and amazement, the station was playing a message for him from his mother back in Canada. The other hostages heard the message too—it was the first proper English they'd heard in two months—and quickly gathered around.

There were three messages in all—one from Barney's mother, another from all the families and a third from United itself.

Barney's mother's message started:

"This is a message to Brant Scheelar.

"All I would like to say is that, Brant, I miss you very much. I will be thinking of you on Halloween and I love you very much. Brant, I hope to see you soon. Please take care of yourself. You are missed by your mother more than you can imagine. I pray for everyone's safe return home. The best to you all. Carolyn."

The hostages erupted. "All right, Barnz!" they said, slapping him on his back. Barney was so choked up, all he could do was grin.

The men heard the message from all the families next.

"There is not a moment that goes by that we do not think of you. Please do not think of us, even though we miss you immensely and are concerned for your well-being. We are coping with the situation. We hope that you will remain strong and that you will support one another."

The message from United was last. It promised "a huge coming-home party with an endless supply of food and drink."

The messages pacified the men and gave them something to think about other than their elaborate plans for escape and retribution. They spent the rest of the day in high spirits.

But the biggest carrot dangled in front of the hostages remained the guerrillas' repeated promises of freedom. Nothing cured the hostages' bitching like a new release date.

On days when the hostages' frustrations bubbled like a kettle of water on high heat, Lario would confide in Rod the newest, revised release date. *"Quince Noviembre"*—November 15—Lario would say to Rod, and the men would cool down. Then, when the mid-November date passed, Lario promised they'd be out by early December. "Negotiations *no finito*, but oh so close," he said.

But the hostages weren't stupid either. Rod knew he was being played with.

This is bullshit. They're feeding us lines. They know we're ready to break so they make us these endless promises, give us a few smokes and then we chill out for a few days. They're yanking our chains and playing with our minds.

Still, there was nothing they could do. The guerrillas were in control.

After Sabine and the Spaniards were released in mid-October, the guerrillas began mentioning a "big *campamento*," a compound across the Colombian border where they claimed 700 Colombian and Ecuadorean policemen and soldiers were being held hostage. The guerrillas bragged of the arsenal of weapons they controlled at the camp—grenade launchers, helicopters, state-of-the-art automatic weapons. The hostages were promised that, after arriving at the *campamento*, they would have their own rooms, with comfortable beds. They could order food off a menu and have unlimited supplies of pop, *cervesas* and cigarettes. They would be allowed access to a telephone so they could contact relatives back home in Edmonton. To get to the compound, the guerrillas would ferry the pipeliners across a huge river—presumably the San Miguel, which separated the two countries—and march them through vast *cocaina* fields. Rod was sure the guerrillas were pumping out more lies; they would never see such grand accommodations.

A much-less hospitable destination was reached at the end of a march in late November. Commandant and Old Tracker had been away from the group for more than a week. Rod hoped this was a sign negotiations with United were back on. In their absence, Hoto and Mr. Tiger Tooth led the way through the bush.

Eventually, they arrived at a patch of thinned-out jungle near a stream, where, to everyone's astonishment, they found Mrs. Tiger Tooth, Commandant and Old Tracker sitting on a log. Mrs. Tiger smiled shyly at the hostages and jumped to her feet to kiss Mr. Tiger Tooth, seemingly fully recovered from the effects of the snake bite.

The guerrillas made it clear that the area—which had none of the creature comforts of the described "big *campamento*"—would be the hostages' new home. The kidnappers went to work knocking down trees to provide clear sight lines to the middle of the camp, where the pipeliners were instructed to erect their tarpaulin shelter under two remaining trees.

Several times, Michael and Goldstar changed into their civilian clothes and left the camp to fetch supplies. After six hours they returned with military knapsacks crammed full of sugar, salt, canned food, packages of rice, powdered cream—everything but meat. The guerrillas, using their machetes and hatchets, had built a table by tying six logs together with rope. Now they piled a mountain of goods on top, as if they were about to open a supermarket in the middle of the jungle.

The hostages, desperate for signs that might indicate their impending release, dissected and interpreted the guerrillas' every move. Perhaps the mass food resupply meant the guerrillas were preparing to free them. If they had to walk days or weeks through the jungle to return to their homes, they'd need lots of food.

But Rod was angry with the kidnappers for neglecting to bring cigarettes.

"We need *cigarrillos*," Rod told Lario after emptying a military backpack so the guerrillas could buy more supplies. "Not all this other crap, *cigarrillos*!"

"*Mañana, mañana*," Lario replied. Tomorrow, tomorrow.

In a few days, Michael and Goldstar relented and picked up a carton of cigarettes. Rod tensed with expectation and jealousy as he watched the guerrillas huddle together to divvy up the bounty. The abductors always got first dibs. Most took two packages of twenty each and tucked them into their vest pockets. The Canadians would get whatever was left, maybe ten cigarettes for the eight of them.

"*Dos* days," a guerrilla said sternly as he handed Rod the hostages' ration. "*Dos* days, *finito*." No more smokes for two days. Rod felt like punching him in the stomach.

At the beginning of the kidnapping, only two guerrillas smoked, Muscles and Mr. Tiger Tooth. But by mid-November, several more had picked up the habit. Most of the new smokers didn't inhale; they simply blew the smoke in and out of their mouths, a habit which enraged Rod.

Though Muscles hardly ever communicated with the Canadians—he still seemed to consider contact with the hostages a professional no-no—occasionally he slid them a few cigarettes from his personal stash. He smoked two packs a day of the strongest brand Rod had ever tried, stronger even than American Marlboros, and much more powerful than the weak brands Michael and Goldstar brought back. Luki, too, bummed smokes off the other guerrillas and handed them over to the North Americans.

"Shhhhh," Luki would say, his index finger over his mouth, as he slipped the pipeliners some extra cigarettes.

"Ahhh, *gracias* Luki. *Gracias*," Rod would whisper with a knowing smile. "You the man, Luki. You the man."

Along with their makeshift log table, the guerrillas also fashioned a bench about five metres from the hostages' tarpaulin shelter so they wouldn't have to stand on guard duty. Two guerrillas sat outside the tent all night in case the hostages harboured any notions of escaping or in case the Ecuadorean army suddenly appeared from behind a hidden glade of trees. After dinner, on the nights the guerrillas were feeling particularly expansive, the oil workers would venture out of their tent and sit on the bench with the guards. The two groups communicated through their stilted mixture of body language, Spanish and English.

The guards were most curious about two things. The first seemed innocuous enough; the kidnappers, especially Lario, wanted to know about Canada and whether the men had families back home. "Friends," Lario would say. "Friends, you, me, *no problemo*, friends. I come to Canada."

"No, Lario, we don't allow machine guns in Canada," Rod replied, laughing.

"Oh, no Canada then."

The second source of the guerrillas' curiosity was more puzzling. They wanted to know if any of the hostages knew how to fly a helicopter. One pointed at Rod, swirling his hands around and around, making chopper sounds. It was akin to playing charades with a five-year-old, but Rod understood.

"No," said Rod, shaking his head. "No, I can't fly a helicopter."

The guerrilla continued to make the helicopter sound and said, "You go *casa?*"

Rod took that as a question about whether the hostages would take a helicopter home to Canada. He shook his head, extended his arms out from his sides and made airplane noises, swooping his torso back and forth as if he were flying through the air. The two smiling guards immediately started chatting excitedly to one another in Spanish as if they had just dawned on a vital realization.

Colin, who was watching the exchange, walked over. "Jesus, Rod, do you know what you just did?" he said.

"I didn't know it at the time, but I think I just told them I know how to fly an airplane."

Why were the guerrillas so keen on knowing whether any of the men were pilots? Rod's mind raced with possibilities and implications. Maybe a helicopter played a part in the negotiations. Once the ransom money was dropped at a predetermined location, the guerrillas might order someone from United's negotiating team to fly a helicopter to a set location and leave. The pipeliners would be directed to the location and ordered to jump into the helicopter and fly it to freedom.

Rod hoped he hadn't screwed things up with his comical miscommunication. The last thing they needed was a release contingent on his ability to fly them out of danger. Unfortunately, there was no sense in trying to make it right with guerrillas. Any attempt to correct the misunderstanding would probably only make matters worse.

As time in the clearing passed, the guerrillas developed an annoying, disgusting habit of relieving themselves directly in front of the hostages' shelter. As the men tried to sleep, the stench of ammonia from the guerrillas' urine would waft under the tarpaulin. Rod asked the guerrillas if they could walk into the bush before urinating, but the kidnappers simply laughed at him. The message was clear: they could piss whenever and wherever they wanted.

In the morning, the hostages covered the area with fresh dirt dug from another area of the clearing. It became a part of the daily routine, one that began every morning, around 6 a.m, with calls of "*Arriba, arriba*, up, up" from their captors.

Rod normally logged only a couple of hours of sleep, kept awake by the rustling of the guerrillas in the bush and the intermittent sound of distant machine-gun fire. Rod would stumble from his hammock and groggily ask Lario or one of the other guerrillas about the shots.

"Colombian military exercise," the guerrillas said. Again, for whatever reason, the kidnappers seemed intent on convincing the pipeliners they were in Colombia. But Rod didn't believe them. The price tags on the supplies were all in *sucre*, Ecuadorean currency, and the precious cigarettes they received had "Ecuador" printed right on the packages. And they hadn't yet crossed the San

Miguel River. Rod was sure they were in Ecuador no matter how much the kidnappers wanted them to believe otherwise.

Upon waking, the men were assaulted by the stench of the soiled patch in front of their tent, and again by the smell of the camp's toilet area further back in the jungle. Everybody in the camp, twenty-two men and Mrs. Tiger Tooth, used the latter several times a day, and the harsh smell made the hostages' eyes water. By mid-afternoon, after the damp ground had hours to ferment in the searing daytime heat, the stench became unbearable.

At 7 a.m., a guerrilla arrived with bowls of steaming coffee for the hostages to share. The aroma was one of the few things the men looked forward to each day. The food was bad, but the coffee was pure Colombian, better than any coffee back home.

Breakfast—nicknamed "rice surprise" by Rod—was served next. It was mostly leftover burnt rice mixed in with whatever the hostages had eaten for supper the night before, usually watery canned tuna, peas or beans. The meal normally arrived around 9:30 a.m, and the men shoved it down, no matter how awful it was. Their next meal wouldn't appear until 5 p.m. Lunch was a rare occurrence.

The guerrillas allowed the hostages to wash their clothes and bathe more often in the creek that ran past the encampment. After scrubbing their clothes in the stream, they hung them in the trees to dry rapidly in the daytime heat. Sometimes the guerrillas ordered the pipeliners to scrub scorched rice out of the giant pots.

The kidnappers bathed in the same stream as the hostages, and Mrs. Tiger Tooth often shed her army jacket and splashed water on her face to cool off. Under her military fatigues, she wore a tiny black shirt that curved tightly around her breasts, revealing her washboard stomach.

Supper was rice and canned tuna or some kind of freshly killed, ill-prepared jungle animal such as monkey or piranha. After force-feeding themselves the main course, the men looked forward to dessert—a pot of coffee or, even better, a concoction of chocolate and boiled water, sometimes containing powdered cream or oats.

After a nighttime smoke, the men changed into their knock-off Nike and Adidas sweats, now filthy and splitting crazily at the seams, and climbed into their hammocks to try to sleep. Every night, Colin prayed out loud before the men drifted off.

"Our Father, who art in Heaven. Hallowed be thy name. Thy kingdom come, thy will be done on earth as it is in Heaven. Give us this day, our daily bread."

Grant and Skunk often joined in. "And forgive us our trespasses as we forgive those who trespass against us. And lead us not into temptation, but deliver us from evil. For thine is the kingdom, the power and the glory, forever and ever, Amen."

Rod, only recently acquainted with God after his near-death experience with his strange illness, prayed quietly to himself. He'd never attended church or Sunday school. But Colin said he could talk to God in plain, simple language and say whatever he wanted.

"God can hear you," Colin told him. "You don't have to go to church. You can make any surrounding area your temple."

A jungle clearing, fetid with the smell of urine and filth, didn't seem like much of a temple to Rod. But he prayed anyway, asking God to look after his family and to get him home alive.

Near the end of November, Rod began the countdown to Christmas. With precious little else to do, he spent hours pondering what he would buy Jane upon his release. Finally he decided on a gold chain to match the one she'd bought him on their wedding day nine years ago. He had less romantic gift ideas, too. A built-in vacuum system topped that list, something sensible to buy with all the cash he made in Fresno and Ecuador before he was captured.

Some of the men borrowed pens and tiny scraps of paper from the guerrillas to scribble down their shopping lists. Rod didn't bother—he planned it all in his head. When he got home, he'd take Jane and Krissy to Las Vegas, get to know his family again.

Rod's reflection in the jungle developed a pattern. Family thoughts inevitably led to him beating himself up over taking the Ecuador trip in the first place. He and Colin talked about the need to re-examine their priorities, about how greed was playing too significant a part in their decision to work away from home ten months out of every year. Rod berated the guerrillas for being money-hungry, but realized his own career had been largely motivated by cash.

He knew it wasn't good for Krissy or Jane for him to be away from home so much. But he'd made the sacrifice in order to stock his home and garage with the best money could buy. He was an easy mark for a salesman trying to make a buck. Now he laughed at himself for being such a fool.

"This experience is going to change me," he explained to Colin. "I'm not going to just blow it off, I'm going to change."

Colin agreed. He told Rod he should never have agreed to spend so much time away from his family. He couldn't bear to think what Karen and his children were going through back home, not knowing if he were alive or dead.

"This is just a job for a company we work for," he said. "I should have stayed home."

Once proud of his buff body and physical appearance, Rod began to notice how much weight he had lost. He figured he'd shed nearly forty pounds, bringing him down to a scrawny 150. All the hostages had lost serious weight; the guerrillas often playfully rubbed their own stomachs, teasing the pipeliners about their lost beer guts.

The men also lost strength and stamina. Now that the night marches had ended, the hostages spent much of the day sitting around in the encampment, either bored silly or fearing the guerrillas' next move. When the kidnappers did order them to walk, sweat would pour off Rod within a half-hour. Two-and-a-half months in the jungle had taken their toll—he was worn out.

Barney, whose once-chubby face looked positively chiselled, now thought his muscles had deteriorated so badly he couldn't imagine lifting, let alone swinging, the sledgehammers he'd hoisted on the pipeline. He felt even worse because his ankle still hadn't healed properly. Barney used a stick as a crutch, looking like an old man when he hobbled about the camp.

The men knew they needed strength, especially if they fell ill or had to resume the gruelling night marches. Skunk and Neil, who came to Ecuador already lean and trim, didn't have much more weight left to lose.

Colin came up with the idea for a homemade chin-up bar, and asked the guerrillas for a rope, which the hostages tied taut between two trees. Colin, Grant and Skunk spent hours hoisting themselves up and down on the rope. Barry, too, gave it a go and impressed his former underlings with his strength, impressive for any man, let alone a worn-down jungle captive in his late-forties. The men complemented this exercise with repeated push-ups on the vine-strewn jungle floor.

A few of the kidnappers were intrigued by the exercise and thought they could show the *gringos* a thing or two. One day, they decided to use the rope, too. The hostages agreed, but on one condition: the guerrillas would have to produce cigarettes as a reward if the Canadians outperformed their captors. The guerrillas agreed and offered the ultimate prize: an entire pack of cigarettes to any man who could do fifteen chin-ups in a row without stopping.

Rod, who'd rarely tried Colin's chin-up bar, now was interested. He couldn't, in good conscience, turn down a shot at a whole pack of cigarettes. "Count me in," he said.

Hoto, the guerrillas' young second-in-command, and Michael, the handsome kidnapper who'd boasted of bedding two *chickilinas* at once, took part. Hoto's strength was particularly impressive. Like many of the other guerrillas, he was small in stature but lean, with rippling muscles and almost no body fat. He often flexed his arms and back as the guerrillas marched along the trails, and did push-ups at the camp on fallen trees to maintain his superior physique. Hoto managed fourteen chin-ups, lowering his body until his arms were straight and then pulling himself up again.

Rod was dying for the chance to show up Hoto. At last, the two sides were on an equal playing field, with machine guns and machetes subtracted from the equation. Rod cupped both hands around the rope and hoisted himself up. He was shocked at how difficult the movement now was—his biceps and forearms, like Barney's, had withered from disuse. He thought he'd better do the exercises quickly, before all his energy was drained. He snapped off a couple chin-ups.

Hoto and Michael screamed that Rod was cheating, and argued that the chin-ups should be done slowly, in a controlled motion, all the way up and then all the way down. He wasn't coming close to straightening his arms before pulling himself back up, they said.

"No, I'm doing it right," Rod said. "You bend your knees and keep your elbows bent so you don't hyper-extend them." The guerrillas relented.

Rod started again. All he could think about was the pack of smokes. His arms trembling, fingers digging into the rope, Rod pulled himself to chin level ten times. But his arms failed him after hitting the eleventh, and he collapsed in the dirt.

Rod vowed to keep trying until he bested Hoto's fourteen chin-ups, but none of the men ever did. Once, Neil hit twelve, and the guerrillas passed out a few cigarettes for his valiant effort. But, just like their release, the prize pack of cigarettes remained an elusive dream.

Despite their acumen and deft handling of the hostages, the guerrillas had been lucky to avoid the Ecuadorean army and the myriad heist-spoiling complications the jungle threw at them. But by late-November, the squalid, debilitating conditions began to have their effect on the guerrillas, too.

The beginning came when Mrs. Tiger Tooth, seemingly fully recovered from her snakebite, rapidly fell ill again.

It was Rod who discovered her one morning after breakfast, sprawled flat on the ground, nestled in the tangled roots of a giant tree. She wasn't sleeping, but lying there in a daze. Rod was astounded. He had no idea how she'd ended up in the tree and wasn't sure what he should do. Should he drag her back to the guerrillas' main tent, or should he go after her weapons and turn them on the rest of the guerrillas?

He was considering the latter option when Mr. Tiger Tooth appeared and approached his young bride. Rod watched as Mr. Tiger Tooth lifted her gently to her feet and led her to the toilet in the bush. She was unsteady on her feet, stumbling over branches and clinging to her husband. The two talked softly as they walked. A few minutes later, Mr. Tiger Tooth led his wife out of the trees. Tears streamed from her bloodshot eyes. She rubbed them constantly as Mr. Tiger Tooth, a mask of worry on his face, led her back to their tent. On the way, she stumbled, as if she couldn't see where she was going.

The revelation hit Rod like a thunderbolt: *Mrs. Tiger Tooth is blind. It must have been the snakebite.*

Later that morning, Rod asked Lario about Mrs. Tiger Tooth's condition, only to be shut down immediately. "No, no," Lario said sternly. "No talk about that."

The following day, Mr. Tiger Tooth walked solemnly up to the hostages and, without a word, gave them a pack of cigarettes. He retrieved his young wife from the tent and led her by the hand away from the camp, accompanied by three guerrillas who carried her machine gun and knapsacks. Again she fell to the ground, and Mr. Tiger Tooth picked her up.

Under normal circumstances, Rod would have felt sympathy seeing a young woman, or anyone, for that matter, struck with blindness. But as he watched Mrs. Tiger Tooth stumble through the bush and out of their lives forever, Rod felt hollow, empty.

I don't care if she dies. It would serve her right.

Mrs. Tiger Tooth's affliction and the dragging on of negotiations had serious effects on the guerrillas' morale. The guerrillas became more unpredictable and increasingly susceptible to the harsh vagaries of jungle life. As the kidnappers grew more erratic, Rod grew more afraid of them.

One morning, Rod heard a blood-curdling scream, and jumped from his hammock under the tarpaulin to see what was happening. He spotted Fabio, howling in pain as he clutched his hand. Fabio's fellow guerrillas rushed toward their injured comrade and emptied out his knapsack. A black scorpion crawled out. Fabio had been bitten by the poisonous insect and his hand instantly started to swell.

Fabio gingerly picked up the scorpion, holding it so it couldn't sting him again, and carried it to Rod. "Very bad," he said, pointing at the dangerous arachnid's pincers and jointed, stinging tail. "*Malo, malo.*" He dropped the fearsome creature on the ground and the guerrillas hacked it to pieces with their daggers, all the while cursing it in Spanish. They dug a hole in the ground and buried the tail, explaining that it could still inject deadly poison if someone accidentally stepped on it.

Fabio, his arm numb to the shoulder, his hand puffy and swollen, was permitted to take a few days off from his duties and took injections to help battle the effects of the poison. But his convalescence did not go over well with Michael, who seemed to think Fabio was overreacting to get out of work. Michael strode past Fabio as the pudgy guard reclined against a log and smashed him in the shoulder with the butt of his machine gun. To add insult to injury, Michael gave Fabio a swift kick in the leg and taunted him. Fabio screamed back, jumping to his feet and grabbing his gun. Rod held his breath as the two guerrillas jammed their machine guns in each other's faces, expecting to hear bursts of fire at any moment. Depending on who pulled the trigger first, Michael or Fabio would be pummelled by thirty-two shells per second, filled with more holes than a pin cushion.

The other guerrillas heard the commotion and ran over to Michael and Fabio. They screamed at the young guards to drop their guns.

Michael and Fabio separated and let their conflict drop, but the tension hung in the air for days. Every time the two guerrillas walked by each other, one would point his gun at the other, clicking the safety on and off.

The conflicts weren't limited to Michael and Fabio. The guerrillas seemed to break down along lines of age and experience. It seemed the younger guerrillas were anxious to take whatever money United was offering. They wanted to strike a deal with United before one of the hostages died. But the older guerrillas, such as Commandant, Muscles and Big Mac, stressed the importance of patience, that negotiations took time.

The two groups squared off during the guerrillas' meetings. Often, the meetings degenerated into screaming matches between the young kidnappers and the old.

Rod didn't know what to make of the split in the group. If the guerrillas turned against each other, how long would it be before the hostages became the targets?

"Holy God," Rod said as he watched the divide widen. "I hope the strong ones are on our side."

A Glimmer of Hope

TOO WEARY TO CRY, too weak to fight, his mind a roiling black ocean, Barney awoke on November 24, Day 75 of the ordeal, at the nadir of his precarious existence in the jungle. He felt like a drowning victim whose head was being held underwater by his murderer. There was no particular event that pushed Barney there, just the relentless battering of his psyche, the overwhelming smells and sounds of seventy-five days of captivity, the soul-crushing sight of his own and his friends' deterioration and the kidnappers' many broken promises. When he awoke, one thought, and one thought only, filled his mind: suicide.

The jungle's thin, dawn light thrust at his eyes, and still lying in his hammock, he looked away from the patch of sky that peeked through the side of the tarpaulin and turned towards the jungle floor, where he saw thousands of ants crawling beneath him. The smell of ammonia wafted from the spot outside the shelter where the guerrillas still insisted on pissing several times a night.

He turned over on his side, and the scabrous, raw skin around his groin split with a piercing crack. He itched from head to toe, covered in insect bites he scratched until they bled.

I'm still in this shithole. There's no way we're ever getting out of here. If only someone took my head off with a machete in the middle of the night. If only the guerrillas would pull me out to the road and put a bullet in my head. Then I wouldn't have to live in this misery a moment longer.

Barney crawled out of his hammock and hobbled outside to brush his teeth, his damaged ankle barely supporting his weight. He needed a doctor to look at it, but that would never happen.

This is the day I'm going to die. This is it. No more burnt rice. No more begging for cigarettes. No more living inside a crowded tent with seven filthy guys. No more dashed hopes after these bastards lie about setting us free.

He limped to the kitchen area, hoping to find Commandant, but found only junior guerrillas on guard duty. The kidnappers said their leader wouldn't be back until later in the day.

That's fine. I'll wait. After seventy-five days, what's a couple of hours?

He walked back to the tent and brushed his teeth. An hour later, he found himself brushing his teeth again, and then again an hour later. It was compulsive; he didn't know why he was doing it. He joked morbidly to himself that at least he'd have healthy dental records so the authorities wouldn't have a problem identifying him when some peasant farmer discovered his rotting corpse dumped on a nearby road.

The other hostages were awake, lounging in their hammocks or playing chess on the borrowed board. But Barney didn't join in; he just paced back and forth, waiting anxiously for Commandant to return. At the heat of midday, he finally spotted the bearded leader strolling towards the guerrillas' makeshift kitchen.

Barney approached Commandant, and in a cool voice, demanded a gun so he could shoot himself in the head.

"*Por favor, por favor,*" Barney said, motioning towards the camouflaged guerrilla's automatic pistol and miming pointing the weapon at his own head. "Please, please. I want this to end."

If I kill myself, I win and you lose. If I'm dead, my nightmare is over and you can't get any money for me.

Commandant just shook his head, which infuriated Barney. This was no joke. It wasn't the same as his request to join the guerrillas so he could help blow up pipelines. He really wanted to shoot himself.

"*Por favor, por favor*," Barney said again, his eyes pleading.

Commandant stared back. "No," he said, in a quiet, firm voice. "No, *loco gringo*." The tall leader had made up his mind, and he walked away. There was no point arguing.

Barney hobbled back to the tent.

"I just asked the Commandant for his gun, and he wouldn't give it to me," Barney said matter-of-factly to the others, as if he'd asked for more cigarettes. "He called me *loco gringo*."

Barney saw his friends shift uncomfortably in their hammocks as if they didn't know what to say. He was almost relieved when Rod broke the ice with a joke. Barney knew humour was the only way any of them could still cope.

"You crazy bastard," said Rod. "When we get home, we're having you committed. They'll put you in a straitjacket the moment you get off the plane. You're not going to have Christmas at home. You'll be in a rubber room while we're all at home eating turkey with our families."

"You won't really tell anybody at home what I did?" Barney asked Rod.

"Bloody right, I'm going to tell them," Rod replied. "We need to have two signatures to have you committed. There are more than two witnesses here, so I'm sure there'll be no problem."

"Well, then, I guess I'll just have to tell them stuff about you too, Rod," said Barney defensively. "You can be in the rubber room with me."

"I've done nothing like what you did," Rod fired back. "You'll be in the rubber room all by yourself on Christmas."

Barney smiled. He knew Rod was looking out for him.

Later, in a quieter moment, Rod told Barney he was at the bottom of a well, but if he craned his neck and looked up far enough, he'd see a ring of light at the top. Rod and the others were halfway up the well, clinging to the side, reaching towards Barney to help pull him out. But Barney had to make the first move: he had to reach up to them.

"It's so close now, Barnz," said Rod. "A matter of days—it's got to be. Now's not the time to be doing something stupid."

Finally, Barney sighed and agreed with his friend.

That night, Barney crawled into his hammock and drifted off to sleep. His dreams this time were not of eviscerating the guerrillas, but of home. Barney saw his mother, father and brother Sean, all crying uncontrollably, dressed in black, sitting in a church. They were at *his* funeral. Barney watched the scene unfold from up above, suspended in the sky where no one could see him.

He listened to his family and friends sing praises of the carefree Barnz they all knew and loved—the prankster, the partier, the hard worker, the caring friend. He watched as his family buried his coffin. But the coffin was empty. His body was somewhere in the jungle, decomposing under a mountain of insects. He hadn't made it home. He'd given up. The guerrillas had won.

Barney awoke the next morning with a new attitude, a new will to live.

I must not give up. I've come too far to back down now.

And then, at last, a glimmer of hope.

In the last week of November, Lario delivered the news the hostages had all but given up hope of ever hearing. The ransom bargaining was *finito*—all that remained was for Barry, whom the guerrillas still considered to be in charge, to speak with a negotiator on the ham radio to confirm the men were still alive.

Rod was in equal parts ecstasy and disbelief. This was incredible news. Finally the hostages would be able to talk to someone from the outside world. But what if the negotiator spoke only Spanish? Barry had never bothered to learn how to communicate with the guerrillas, so his conversation with United's negotiator would not move past "*No espagnol, no espagnol.*"

The other men motioned wildly with their hands at Rod, imploring him to talk to Lario to fix this potential disaster. Rod approached Lario and asked:

"*Dos* of us? *Dos* of us talk on the radio?"

Lario liked Rod, but this time he wouldn't budge. He shook his head, turned his back, and resumed his attempt to communicate the plan to Barry. But Rod continued to pester Lario. In his best broken Spanish, he told Lario this was their only chance to get out. They didn't want a language barrier to screw it up. But Lario still would have none of it. He whirled around and glared at Rod, before turning back to Barry. The message was clear: Barry was the one the guerrillas and United negotiators wanted on the radio.

Rod trudged back to the tent and shrugged his shoulders. "I tried," he said to his fellow captives. "But I'm not about to argue with someone with a machine gun."

Rod immediately switched his focus to discussing strategy with Barry, who, for once, was receptive to his advice. He wanted Barry to ask what was taking so long and why United was having problems coming up with the money. He wanted Barry to make it clear that the men wanted—no, demanded—the company pay the ransom and pay it now.

Barry told Rod he'd pass the message on if the man on the radio was Ken Foster, Rob Mackie, or another United official who spoke English. But Barry didn't know what he'd do if the negotiator on the other end spoke only Spanish.

The foreman sat in his hammock with a faraway look in his eyes and Rod knew he was concentrating; he knew Barry was painfully aware the hostages' fate was in his hands. Rod also wondered if Barry was hoping this was his chance to make amends for the trouble he'd caused them in the jungle.

The next morning, the hostages waited for the guerrillas to summon Barry. But, as morning bled into afternoon and afternoon faded into evening, there was still no news from the kidnappers. Rod sat outside the tarpaulin tracking the guerrillas' movements like a hawk, searching for signals that the time was near. The wait was agonizing; Rod's mind swirled with impatience and hope. At sunset, Lario and a few of his comrades disappeared with the radio and the antenna, but they didn't take Barry with them.

When Lario returned, Rod bombarded him with questions. "What's going on? Why didn't you get Barry? When will we go home?" Lario shook his head and offered no answers.

Finally, after Rod spent a near-sleepless night tossing and turning in his hammock, the next morning brought with it more news. At breakfast, Lario walked over to the pipeliners and announced that the plan had been changed. Barry would no longer be the hostages' representative. Instead, all the men would get the chance to tell the negotiator—and the world—they were still alive.

Lario ordered the pipeliners to write out a message to a family member other than their wives or their mothers. The letter was to contain a secret message—something only the family member would understand. Lario kept saying, "Personal, personal," over and over. Rod decided to write his note to his older sister Connie.

On another sheet, Lario told them to copy down their home addresses. Rod wasn't happy about telling the guerrillas where he lived, but he did not argue for fear of screwing up the process.

At 4 p.m. the guerrillas delivered a pot of rice and green peas and told the men to hurry. Rod was so excited he could hardly eat and he could tell the kidnappers' minds were elsewhere. The guerrillas didn't bring the traditional after-dinner bowl of coffee or take the rice pot away. An hour later, Lario approached the hostages and said: "*Vamoose, vamoose.* Radio."

The guerrillas led the oil workers from the camp through the jungle until they hit a wide stream. Rod lost his balance on the crossing log and splashed into the stream, but somehow managed to stick his arm up and keep his cigarette dry. He walked out of the stream, soaking wet, holding his smoke in the air in celebration as if he had just scored a Stanley Cup–winning overtime goal. Lario applauded Rod's feat, smiled at the redheaded Canadian and handed him another cigarette.

After the group teetered across the stream, they broke trail a short distance through the jungle, eventually stopping at a grassy clearing. The open space, evidently, was the best place within a several-kilometre radius to send and receive ham-radio transmissions.

The atmosphere in the clearing was charged, almost party-like. Both groups, the hostages and guerrillas alike, were beginning to believe they might make it home for Christmas. They chatted easily to one other as Lario, the communications expert, fiddled with the radio. The kidnappers were in a playful mood—some of the younger ones darted around the clearing like hyperactive children, chasing Congo ants on logs and wrestling one another. The tension, taut as a hangman's noose just two days before, seemed temporarily to have evaporated.

Rod thought he even felt a subtle power shift in the clearing. For the first time in more than two months, the hostages would have a say in the outcome of the situation. The guerrillas seemed to know that all their efforts—and their multi-million ransom— came down to this very minute, to a successful communication with United's negotiators. For once, the guerrillas actually seemed nervous around the hostages, instead of the opposite.

Lario and his comrades took the radio out of its box, hooked it to a bulky car battery and attached a piece of wire for an antenna. They chopped down a slim tree with a machete, tied the antenna to the top of the trunk and stood the tree back up.

Lario played with the radio's buttons, manipulating the frequencies, as he stared down at his watch. Finally, across the ether, came a distant voice, speaking in Spanish. This was surely the United negotiator, but Rod's heart sank. What if the man didn't speak English? What if the communications got screwed up?

Then an epiphany.

Through the crackling static, Rod heard the beautiful, heart-stopping words: "Can I speak to Brant Scheelar, please?"

Rod, grinning ear-to-ear, cranked his head round to look at his friend but Barney was already on his feet, rushing toward the spot on the log where Lario sat with the radio. He grabbed the microphone out of Lario's hand and replied: "My name is Brant Scheelar."

The negotiator, an Ackerman rep using the codename Juan, told Barney he'd fetched personal questions from all the hostages' families back in North America. Only the pipeliners would know the answers.

Juan asked Barney: "Your mother's father had a dog buried out on the acreage. What was the breed of the dog and the dog's name?"

Barney was quick to answer: "The dog's name was Princess and it was a golden retriever."

Juan then told Barney he should read his prepared message, the one only his family back home would understand. Barney said: "Hi. This is Brant Scheelar. Hello, Dad. Tell everybody I'm safe. Tell everybody I love them. Looking forward to your mooseburgers. I can't wait to come home so I can rebuild the Express." The Express was the 1979 L'il Red Express truck in his father's driveway.

"Excellent, excellent Brant," Juan said. "I'll see you guys in a few days. We're going to get you out of there as soon as possible."

Barney sat down on a nearby log, shaking, trying to light a cigarette, nearly overcome by the first English conversation he'd had with the outside world in almost eighty days.

The other hostages answered their questions in turn, wanting desperately to supply the correct information. They nervously whispered amongst themselves: What if I give the wrong answer? What if only one person screws up? Would they be left behind?

Rod tried to calm the group down. "It's not like they're going to say 'This isn't you' and hang up. If they talk to seven out of the eight and you get your question wrong, they'll know it's you. They'll know it's not one of the guerrillas, because you speak good English."

Still Rod did not want to be the one to mess up.

Just get it right. Speak clearly, answer the question correctly and we'll all get to go home.

Just then, the radio crackled and faded and Lario ordered the Ackerman rep to switch frequencies. "Venezuela, Venezuela," Lario barked into the microphone. The other guerrillas stood around anxiously.

After a suspenseful pause, Juan's voice finally filtered through again. Juan asked to speak to Rod.

"My name is Rod Dunbar," Rod said into the microphone, and then proceeded to read his note to Connie.

"Hi Sis," he said. "I'm doing OK. Say hi to everybody for me. Be home soon. Say hi to Tweet for me." Only his family would know the bit about Tweet, Krissy's infant name. How proud his daughter would be to know she helped get him out of the jungle alive.

"It's very good to hear from you, Rod," the voice over the radio crackled. "My name is Juan. I'm here to help you get out. How is your health?"

"My health is good," Rod replied, minding Lario's orders to refrain from talking about being sick, the bad food or anything regarding the camp's conditions. "I'm doing OK."

"OK, Rod," Juan said. "I have an important question from your family. You had a dog that recently died. What was her name and what breed was she?"

"Her name was Baby," Rod said, "and she was a German shepherd/wolf cross."

"You did very good, Rod. Very good. We will see you very soon."

Rod trembled as he walked back to the log. "Thank God, I got it right," he whispered to Barney. "I was shitting bricks before, but I feel pretty good now."

More questions from Juan followed. Steven's question was: "You and your brother used to jump from a bridge. Who would jump first?" Leonard was asked what colour the door was on his Ford truck back on the Navajo reservation.

Juan asked Grant the name of a grandparent on his father's side, but Grant was so nervous he blurted out the wrong family member. There was silence on the other end.

"I'm going to repeat the question, Grant," Juan said. "I said a relative on your father's side. What did you call him? What was his name?"

Grant's eyes lit up and he said the correct answer.

"You did very, very well, Grant," Juan said. "You answered the question very well."

After all the hostages were questioned, Juan and Lario spoke briefly to each other, and the communication ended.

As the guerrillas and hostages marched back to camp in the dark, each group was jubilant for their own reasons. The guerrillas knew the negotiations were close to being complete, and United would soon shower them with riches beyond their wildest dreams. For the hostages, it was the first concrete step toward freedom they'd had in months.

In all the excitement, the kidnappers remembered to bring only one flashlight. During the walk back to the camp, the captors and captives alike stumbled over tree branches and took wrong turns in the bushes, but the guerrillas didn't seem at all worried the pipeliners would run off. Lario kept saying, "Soon, you go *casa*. Soon, you *vamoose*."

Upon returning to the camp, the guerrillas made a pot of coffee for the men. Soon after, the hostages turned in for the night. Rod wondered how he'd be able to relax enough to sleep after the talk with Juan. But he needn't have worried. For the first night in ages, Rod slept without waking until dawn.

———

Back in Edmonton, Jane struggled to put up a brave face despite her growing fear she might never see Rod again.

Jane and Krissy threw themselves into packing a personalized care package for Rod. United still believed the kidnappers were FARC. In the past FARC had accepted care packages from family members delivered by the Red Cross.

Jane shopped for deodorant, travel-sized shampoo, a comb, Band-Aids, cotton swabs, and mosquito repellent. She also tucked in a tube of antibiotic cream and a container of aspirin. Figuring Rod might be bored, she added a hand-held Yahtzee video game. Her brother Bruce contributed a few snowmobile magazines.

United encouraged the hostages' families to write letters, but advised them to keep the messages short. The guerrillas likely couldn't read English well and would probably toss out the letters that proved too difficult to translate. The printing was to be large and easily legible so the kidnappers could scrutinize the contents.

Krissy drew a picture of herself for Rod and attached a note:

"To Daddy,

"I miss you. I hope you come home real soon. We think about you all the time. I love you. You are on the news.

"Love, Tweet (Krissy)"

She drew a heart at the bottom of the page.

Jane struggled with her letter. She had so much to say, but no idea how to say it. Her first draft was much too long—four pages, single-spaced. She scrapped it, knowing the guerrillas would probably throw it away.

She tried again:

"*Dear Rod,*

"*I love you and miss you more than I can put into words. Krissy and I are doing OK. But our lives have only one focus and that is to have you here with us. The truck/house and everything is OK, so only think about you, your health and coming home.*

"*Love always, Jane and Krissy*"

She thought twice about mentioning Rod's truck but she knew he would worry about how she was managing, and wanted to put his mind at ease.

Jane tried to prepare for Christmas as if it were a normal year. Christmas was always a huge deal at the Dunbar house, and she wasn't about to change. She hung decorations in every room on the house, and started putting up the Christmas tree.

All the ornaments were on the tree when Jane reached for the angel to place on top. But Krissy objected. Rod always hoisted Krissy high into the air so she could place the angel on the top branch. Now she told Jane the angel must stay down until Daddy got home. Jane agreed and put the angel on the shelf, silently praying the cherub would make it to the top branch before Christmas.

Jane went shopping for Rod's birthday, which fell on December 2. She decided to give him a gold bracelet to match the gold chain she'd given him on their wedding day. The bracelet would be a reminder of the time they'd been separated and a reminder that the kidnappers couldn't keep them apart.

For Christmas, Jane bought Rod a hammock for the backyard. It was not unlike the one Rod slept on every night in the jungle.

At the end of November, Jane heard from Sabine Roblain, who was now back with her family near Montreal.

Sabine told Jane stories about how Rod talked incessantly about selling the truck in Fresno. He'd even joked about selling it to the guerrillas once the ordeal was over.

That's Rod, thought Jane. Even at gunpoint in the jungle, he's thinking about selling something and making a buck. She felt better, knowing Rod still had it in him to joke and laugh. Sabine added that Rod was keeping mentally strong for the sake of the other guys that many of them seemed to take their emotional cues from him. That made Jane proud, too.

Jane and Sabine also talked about the frustrations of dealing with the media, who were still keen on digging up information about the hostage-taking.

Jane still refused to speak to reporters, but was frustrated by the inaccurate stories they occasionally ran. On December 2, Rod's birthday, the *Edmonton Journal* quoted an Ecuadorean newspaper report that said Rod and the others had already been released. Jane knew from Ken Foster and Foreign Affairs officials that this simply wasn't true, yet countless friends and family members called to congratulate her. Neighbours knocked on the door to share in the celebrations, only to be told the bad news by Jane.

Jane wanted to call *The Journal* to chastise them for printing the story, but she knew United would be angry with her, and so would the other families.

Jane did the only thing she could think of, calling a nearby Wal-Mart to ask if she could set up a table there over the weekend. The store said she could, so Jane sat by the entrance and told anyone who would listen that her husband and the other hostages were still very much in captivity, and that *The Journal* was wrong. She asked people to sign a "Welcome home" card for the men when they finally *did* come home. Dozens of people stopped to sign the cards.

"We will be so glad to have you back," one woman wrote. "Thank God for all things. There was a reason for this. God bless you. Welcome home."

Surprisingly, though, some took exception to Jane's cause. One hostile customer said the workers deserved to be taken hostage for all the damage done to the fragile Latin American environment by

North American oil companies. He said the pipeliners were getting a just payback for their own greed.

"They shouldn't have been there in the first place," he said. "What the hell did they think they were doing? What else could you expect?"

In the past, Jane had questioned the nature of Rod's work. Perhaps money was driving her husband to spend too much time away from home. But she couldn't stomach the suggestion that he deserved to be kidnapped. That was too much and she snapped at the customer.

"They're supporting their families, what do you think they're doing?" she yelled at the man.

Jane walked out of the store to regain her composure. She didn't want to create a scene and get kicked out before the cards were signed.

But the man followed Jane out the door, continuing his tirade. By now, Jane had had enough. She yelled at him, called him an "uncaring asshole" and kept up her barrage until he got in his car and left.

She couldn't believe the nerve of the man, but for the first time in weeks, she felt strong.

Ghost Stories

BY THE END OF November, Rod's life in the jungle was a tapestry of conflicting emotions, highs and lows woven together and stitched with long, long threads of suffocating boredom. After speaking with Juan on the radio Rod felt invincible, as though he and the other men had won their little small-scale jungle war against the guerrillas. Within days they would be released—for real, this time. Rod started to hatch reunion plans and revised his mental lists for Christmas gifts and favoured holiday destinations. Freedom became a palpable thing, as visible and reachable as the treed horizon spied from a jungle hillside.

But, as more promised release dates continued to come and go, he became despondent again. The story line became predictable. Commandant and one or two of his lieutenants—Hoto, usually, or Muscles—would leave the camp, presumably to finally settle the negotiations. The remaining kidnappers would tell the pipeliners they'd be freed upon his return. But Commandant would appear back at the camp with no news, and the hostages would be held captive for yet another week. Each time it was like a little one-act play, and the denouement—the moment when Rod and the others, frustrated and furious, realized they weren't going home—was always crushing.

The Canadians tried to keep their spirits up with more chess games and more chin-up sessions and then, as the calendar flipped over into December, with Rod's ghost stories.

Every night, after a dinner of rice and chicken, or rice and fish, or rice and beans, the guerrillas served coffee and the pipeliners, excited as little children, retired to their hammocks underneath Ghost Stories the tarp to listen to Rod spin stories of spectres and spirits. Barry didn't like them—"No fucking ghost stories after seven o'clock!" he'd growl—but everyone else did, and the majority ruled.

A lousy raconteur at home—he was always forgetting the punch lines to jokes and getting the characters screwed up—Rod somehow hit his storytelling stride in the jungle. One could joke that it was because he had a captive audience. And the spooky atmosphere was tailor-made. The wind whistled through the tree-tops, mimicking the faint cries of the monkeys, perfectly accentuating Rod's slow, deliberate delivery.

One night, the men gave their eight supper bowls back to the guerrillas and crammed together in their hammocks. Neil, who snored so loudly the guerrillas often ducked under the tarpaulin to shake him awake, was at one end, followed by Leonard, Barry, Skunk, Barney and Grant. Rod and Colin tied their hammocks above the other six, so the narrow tarp would protect all eight men from the nightly rains. They were jammed together uncomfortably close, but it was so dark they couldn't see no matter how well their eyes adjusted. The only light came from the glowing ember of a shared cigarette.

Rod told one of his favourite stories.

"This one's about the little girl in the window," Rod said.

Someone moved in their hammock and let out a scared, expectant little squeal.

That would be Colin, Rod thought. He's probably pulling his blanket over his head and hiding like he always does.

Outside, the hostages could hear the telltale clicks and clacks of the guerrillas breaking down and cleaning their machine guns. The kidnappers didn't need ghost stories; they had real enemies to prepare for.

Rod ignored the sound and started the story, the one about the little girl in the window.

"A young couple, a guy and his wife, pretty wealthy people, move into this beautiful, Cape Cod style house by the sea on Prince Edward Island. He's a newspaperman and he ends up getting a job at the local newspaper in town. But before he starts his job, they move into the house and start unpacking. It's a huge house, two stories, five bedrooms. They don't have enough furniture to fill all the bedrooms, so they just use the one master bedroom and a couple of other bathrooms upstairs.

"They start to get settled in and the welcome wagon starts dropping by, other couples with casseroles and stuff. Some of the neighbours bring their kids with them. They say, 'Hi, nice to meet you, how are you doing?' And some of them, the ones with kids, say, 'Is your daughter home? We brought our kids and they'd like to meet your daughter.'

"The new couple look at each other and say, 'Um, we don't have a daughter. We don't have any children. We just got married.'

"The neighbours look at each other, but don't say anything. They figure they must have made a mistake.

"But a couple of days later, another neighbour comes by and brings his kids with him, too. They meet and the neighbour says, 'My kids came over to play with your daughter.'

"The husband says, 'That's the strangest thing. You're the second person to say that. We don't have any children. Where have you seen this girl?'

"'We've seen her on several occasions, whenever we drive by the house in the afternoon,' the neighbour says. 'The last time was today, about four o'clock. We drove by and she was standing up in the upstairs bedroom window, waving to us as we drove by in our car. A little girl in a white dress.'

"The husband and wife look at each other. She says, 'That's impossible. We never use that bedroom and we don't have any children. It must have been one of the neighbourhood kids who got into the house and was snooping around.'

"The neighbour let it go, but it nagged at the couple. The next day, the husband gets off work early and drives home around four o'clock. He parks his car across the street and watches the window for signs of the girl. Nothing happens. He says to himself, 'Ahh, this is ridiculous' and he pulls into his driveway.

"Just as he gets out of his car, he hears something and glances up. Bang, there's a little girl in the window, smiling at him and waving. He slams the car door, runs into the house and grabs his wife.

"'Come on out here, quick!' he says. 'You've got to check this out right now.' They run into the yard, look up to the window and sure enough, there's the little girl looking straight down at them."

Just then, as Rod paused to catch his breath, a gust of wind tore through the encampment, felling a large tree barely thirty metres from the hostages' shelter. It crashed to the ground with an enormous snap, stripping tree branches during its long fall. The hostages jumped in their hammocks.

"Holy shit, that was close!" one of them whispered.

"Maybe it took out one of the guerrillas," Rod laughed, and continued his story.

"Where was I? Oh, yeah. The guy and his wife are in the yard, looking up at the window, and the husband says, 'OK, you wait here. Keep an eye on that kid. I'm going to run up to the room and grab her and find out whose daughter this is. We can't have someone's kid running around our house.'

"So he runs up the stairs, throws open the door to the bedroom, but there's no girl. He looks around, sees a couple of stacks of books underneath the window sill, but no girl. He walks over to the window, reaches down to open it so he can ask his wife if he has the right room. He looks down at his wife, and, as soon as she sees him, she faints. Boom, over she goes.

"He freaks. He runs out of the room, back down the stairs, outside to his wife. He grabs her, sits her up, kind of shakes her awake. 'What happened to you?' he says. 'You passed out. Are you all right?'

"The wife says, 'Well, didn't you see her?'

"'See who?' the husband says. 'There was nobody there. I went to the window and looked straight down at you. You were looking right at me.'

"'No, no, no,' she says. 'She was right in front of you. You had your arms around her.'

"'There was nobody else in that room,' he says. 'Look, I'll prove it to you.' He grabs his wife's hand, drags her up the stairs. She's really scared, doesn't want to go into the bedroom, but he pulls her in. As soon as they get through the door, the stacks of books underneath the window fall over.

"'What was that?' the wife asks.

"'It was just a vacuum or something from coming through the door,' he says. 'I told you there was nobody up here. We were both seeing things.'

"Then his wife walks over to the books and starts digging through the piles. She gets to the top book and turns white. Then she looks at the top book on the other pile and starts to cry.

"'What's wrong?' the husband says.

"The wife holds up both books. They're covered in dust, but in the dust on each book is a shoe print, a tiny, little girl's shoe print."

Rod was finished. He sat in his hammock, soaking up the hushed silence. "So?" he said.

"Jesus, Rod," Colin moaned. "Thanks a lot. We're in the middle of the jungle, surrounded by people with machine guns, and you're scaring the shit out of us. Thanks."

"Well," Rod said, "do you want me to stop then or do you want to hear another one?"

A pause. Then laughter from Colin. "Another one. Tell another one."

When Rod wasn't scaring the other men with ghost stories, he was terrorizing Grant, whose near-pathological fear of insects was worsened by the ant attack on Leonard. Grant was afraid ants or caterpillars would get into his hammock so, every night, just as the men started to drift off, Rod took something—a balled up leaf, a tiny clump of dirt—and dropped it on Grant below.

One night, Rod took a stick, leaned down quietly and scratched the side of Grant's hammock.

Grant shuddered and slapped at the stick, fearing it was the beginning of an infestation. "Rod, are you fucking with me?" he said.

"No, man, what are you talking about? I'm up here," Rod replied.

He waited five minutes for Grant to settle back down, then leaned back over and scratched Grant's hammock again.

It elicited the same reaction: Grant flailed at the phantom swarm and said, "Are you sure you're not scratching the side of my hammock?"

"No! Now shut the hell up and go to sleep."

Another five minutes passed. Rod leaned over again, listening for Grant's slow breathing. He poked Grant's hammock with the stick yet again.

This time, Grant screamed, flipped right out of his bed and landed on the ground. The other men, all in on the joke, erupted in laughter.

In the early days of the ordeal, the guerrillas would have responded to such hijinks with drawn machetes or threatened gunshots to the head. But as the weeks wore on, the kidnappers let the hostages get away with more.

Most importantly, they now let them wander unguarded down to the stream to bathe or clean their clothes whenever they wanted. But even bathing had its dangers in the middle of the jungle. The guerrillas often polluted the creek with buckets of chicken guts, leftover burned rice and other garbage. Rod worried he'd catch something from the raw animal waste, but the stream's cold water was too refreshing to refuse.

One afternoon, the creek's cool allure nearly cost Leonard his life. Leonard went to the creek to bathe. Minutes later, a deafening shotgun blast reverberated throughout the encampment. The hostages jumped to their feet and ducked under the tarpaulin into the clearing but the guerrillas were already halfway to the stream. One of them ordered Rod and the others to stay still while they investigated.

Suddenly Leonard appeared, running from the direction of the creek. The shotgun blast had missed him by six feet, he said, his complexion ghost-white despite his dark skin.

Military! Rod thought. Jesus Christ, here we go!

The guerrillas slithered down to the creek and to Rod's surprise, he soon heard talking, conversation, not barked orders. The guerrillas had discovered a nearby rancher's children out hunting; one of them had fired the shot at Leonard, perhaps mistaking the American for a jungle cat or boar. The kidnappers sent the children away with a warning: Don't come back and don't tell anyone we're here.

In early December, with many of the hostages nearly crippled by constipation and stomach pains, the guerrillas brought into camp a tried-and-true remedy: beer. The guerrillas told Rod that the beer would loosen up the hostages' clogged systems and help them go to the bathroom.

The guerrillas had purchased twenty-four cans of Poker, a brand of Colombian beer. Each pipeliner got two cans in the late morning just as the sun's rays reached their fullest intensity. Before downing his brews, Rod walked to the stream—thankfully not as polluted with chicken intestines and leftover rice as most days—and bathed. He walked back to the ground in front of the tarpaulin, lit a cigarette, and popped the Poker's top.

He drank, remembering a scene from the movie *The Shawshank Redemption*, a prison drama about a wrongfully convicted accountant, Andy Dufresne. In the scene, Andy and his con friends are tarring the prison roof when Andy overhears the head guard—a mean son-of-a-bitch who beats the prisoners whenever they dare utter a contrary word—lamenting how the taxman is ripping him off. Andy, seemingly apropos of nothing, asks the guard if he trusts his wife, and is nearly thrown from the roof for his trouble. But, dangling over the roof in the head screw's angry grasp, Andy manages to explain that the guard can save money by setting up a tax shelter for his wife. Andy agrees to set up the shelter on one condition: the guard has to bring the prisoners three beers each, and grant them a break from tarring the roof. The guard agrees, and as the men drink, the narrator says that the prisoners, for the first time in decades, feel like free men.

Rod and the others clinked cans. They didn't exactly feel like free men. But, as the alcohol did its magic on their bodies and the sun warmed their faces, at least for a while they felt human.

During the booze-free days, the men passed the time playing chess and cards, or leafing through Ecuadorean newspapers the kidnappers had discarded, while the guerrillas watched from their tents around the perimeter. Once, without asking the guerrillas, Barney went over to the guerrillas' portable camp kitchen.

"What the hell are you doing, Barnz?" asked Rod.

"Just going to make some coffee," he said, as if he had the run of the place. The guerrillas sat with bemused looks as the big Canadian heated up the Coleman stove and brewed up a fresh pot.

One afternoon in early December Barney nearly pushed Chemaisu, the acne-scarred, heavy metal-loving guerrilla, too far. Although the hostages and guerrillas had their lighter moments together—congenial chess matches, English/Spanish lessons, drunken boasts about ménages à trois—their relationships were hardly friendly. Barney and Chemaisu were particularly hostile to each other. Their enmity stretched back to mid-October when Barney battled his mystery illness. Chemaisu approached the Canadian and motioned at Barney's watch, the Heineken timepiece Jesus had traded him. With hand motions and broken English, Chemaisu told Barney he planned to bury the Canadian when he died. But before he filled in the grave, he would snatch the Heineken watch from Barney's corpse. Even in his weakened state, Barney felt like strangling the bastard.

The present incident had to do with food, though, not watches. The guerrillas were feeding the hostages only oats and cold water for lunch, and the meagre meals didn't change the day Chemaisu was cooking.

Barney ate the food, a pasty gruel that did nothing to satisfy his appetite, and was desperate for more. Barney asked Lario, the guerrillas' softest touch, for anything, even an extra bag of oats.

Lario shook his head and told Barney he'd have to talk to Chemaisu. Chemaisu said, "No, no, no," and wagged his index finger at Barney.

Barney pleaded with Lario some more. Finally, Lario jogged over to the kitchen, plucked a bag of oats from a tree stump that doubled as a table, and gave it to Barney.

Chemaisu lost it. He jumped up and down, threw utensils around the camp, picked up his machine gun and pointed it at Lario.

Jesus, Barney thought. If he's going to shoot his own, he's definitely going to shoot me. He ducked for cover, still cradling his bag of oats.

Lario may have been clumsy, perhaps even a bit clownish, what with his propensity for losing contact lenses and misplacing his machine gun, but he was strong as an ox. He swatted Chemaisu's weapon out of his face and chastised the younger guerrilla for being an idiot. Then, to rub it in, he gave the hostages some chocolate to mix in with the oats.

Later in the day, while the men sat around under their tarpaulin, their hunger dulled for the time being, Chemaisu approached the group, and spat something in Spanish at Barney.

"What's that?" Barney snapped.

Chemaisu didn't reply, but he put his gun down, balled his hands into fists and motioned for Barney to stand up. It was a challenge—Chemaisu wanted to fight.

Barney darted out from under the tarpaulin, growling at Chemaisu: "You want a piece of me? Come on, then. Let's go," and thundered across the clearing toward the guerrilla like a bull charging a red flag.

But before Barney could get near him, Chemaisu turned on his heels, casually picked up his gun, glowered at Barney and walked away.

They're pushing me, to see how far I'll go. Goddamn mind games.

December 9 dawned with yet another promise that the hostages were about to be freed. Commandant was away from the camp, Lario said, but when he returned in the afternoon, the hostages' ordeal would be over.

But as the day wore on, the guerrillas did not move to pack up their food and equipment, and mentioned nothing to the hostages about the route they were to take to civilization. The afternoon passed. It became clear Commandant was not coming back as promised.

The realization set Barney off again.

For weeks, he'd been formulating a plan for his own escape. The suicide attempt had failed. Cajoling Old Tracker into giving him a gun had not worked. But an escape just might. He was too angry to realize his scheme was as badly flawed as his own deteriorating mental state.

In the late afternoon, in the last hours of hazy daylight, Barney dug through his belongings and put on all the camouflage gear he had. He smeared his face with mud, obscuring his white skin. What he was about to do would require military precision, and Barney would do it full-on, guerrilla-style.

Barney took a half-dozen two-litre water bottles down to the creek and filled them. Rage and frustration welled inside him. But he forced himself to appear calm. Otherwise, the guerrillas might sense his anger and close in on him.

Barney took the water bottles back to the tarpaulin, and without a word to the other men, placed the heavy containers in his hammock. He wedged sticks in under the bottles, propped the sides of the hammock out and placed his blanket over the top. The illusion was complete; to the guerrillas or any other observers, it appeared as though he was in his hammock, fast asleep.

As Barney smoothed his blanket to perfect the deception, Rod whispered to him:

"Don't be doing nothing stupid, Barnz. Don't be doing nothing dumb. We're too close to the end now."

Barney didn't even look up. "Oh, no problem," he said, the sunny tone in his voice as phony as his face paint. He walked outside and stretched his legs, limbering up for what was to come. Stealthily, on tip-toe, he walked back down to the creek, near the guerrillas' cooking area. None of the guerrillas were in sight; they were playing chess or talking under the main tent.

Then Barney spotted what he was looking for—a machine gun and knife one of the guerrillas had carelessly left behind. He would snatch them and shoot his way out. Barney squatted by the creek, waiting for the right moment.

But as his pulse raced, doubt flooded his mind.

Should I do it? How many guerrillas can I reasonably expect to kill? Two? Three? Eight? How would I be able outrun any of them, with my bum ankle? Say I do peg off a half dozen of them. Say I do get to Tarapoa, or Lago Agrio. What will the guerrillas do? Will they

kill any of the other guys to set an example? No, that's the wrong ques-
tion. The question is: How many of the other guys will they kill?

Barney heard footsteps approach from behind. He wheeled on his haunches, expecting to see Chemaisu or one of the other guerrillas, pissed off and ready to belt him one for wandering off without permission.

But it wasn't one of the guerrillas; it was Barry.

Barney was surprised to see him. He could see Rod coming down to the creek to talk him out of running, or maybe Grant. But after his huge fight with Barry back in September, Barney figured his boss didn't give a shit about him.

"Hey, Barney," said Barry. "What's going on down here?"

"I've had enough, man," Barney said, looking down the creek bed where it snaked and burbled deeper into the jungle. "I'm ready to go."

"Hey, man, don't do it. We're all going to get out of here together," Barry said. "Come on up, we'll talk about it. Nothing can be that bad."

But Barney wasn't buying it. He listed off a litany of grudges he had against the guerrillas. He talked about how his heart ached at being away from home. He talked about how furious he was that his freedom and independence had been stripped from him.

Barry understood; he felt the same way. But he told Barney that running wouldn't solve anything.

"Say you did get a gun. Would you even know how to use it?"

Barney allowed that he probably wouldn't.

Barry told Barney about his plans after they were released. He was thinking of moving to Durango, Colorado to take a job at United's head office. It was a great promotion—big money, not as much time on the road, more of an administrative thing. He told Barney he'd put in a good word for him with United when they got out.

"You've got a good future to look forward to. Don't ruin it by doing something stupid now."

Finally, after about fifteen minutes, the two men, the boss and the grunt, their time in the jungle charged with acrimony, worked it out by the creek's edge, then returned to the tarpaulin. The other men greeted them quietly. Barney removed the water bottles from the hammock, cleaned himself up, and shuffled over to the area they called the guard shack, where two sentry guerrillas kept an eye on things. He sat there, too ashamed to face the others, for the rest of the day, thinking about how close he'd come to taking a bullet in the back.

He remembered how Rod and Colin tried to carry him after he snapped his ankle, and how Rod hauled him down to the creek when he was burning with fever. Guilt washed over him like light rain.

Those guys saved my life, and I was ready to put them in danger.

After a few hours of reflection, he walked back to the tarpaulin.

"I was ready to bolt there, boys," he said.

Rod grinned at his friend and said: "Barney, you wouldn't know where to run. With your sense of direction, you'd do a figure eight and run right back to the camp!"

The guys started to laugh, Barney hardest of all.

"If you do run, Barnz," Rod continued, "when the bullets start flying, don't zig or zag. Do the serpentine."

At that the men broke into howls of laughter. Rod was braying so hard he felt like he was about to throw up.

Several kidnappers, drawn by all the commotion, stared hard at the hostages, wondering whether they were going crazy.

Perhaps, in a way, they were.

Three Bangs on a Tree

IT TURNED OUT there was a good reason for Commandant's extended absence from the camp in early December—he, Vladimir and the Old Tracker had marched several kilometres away to fetch the ransom.

The settlement was reached on December 2, after Gord Black returned to Vancouver for a much-needed break. RCMP Corporal John Tost, a negotiator who didn't have Gord's international anti-terrorist training but had years of hostage-negotiating experience in Canada, arrived in Quito to help advise the Ackerman men. The negotiators had whittled down the guerrillas' ransom demand bit by bit until the two sides reached a deal—$3.5 million U.S. The terms of the release were these: a nun and a priest, both of them humanitarian-minded Catholic church leaders well-known in Lago Agrio, would walk to a predetermined jungle clearing outside the Sucumbios capital with the money. There, the United workers would be released and the guerrillas would disappear back into the jungle, without fear of a military ambush or other reprisals.

The clergy offered to help, as they had in previous hostage tak-ings in South America, because guerrilla groups, both left-wing and right, were often deeply religious, and the Catholic church was one institution both sides could trust.

The nun and the priest carried the money into the clearing on December 3, and were met there by Commandant, Vladimir and

Old Tracker. The guerrillas took the money but did not produce the hostages. The church's representatives asked where the Canadian pipeliners were.

The guerrillas said they'd lied to the negotiators, that the hostages were nowhere near the clearing. They claimed they needed time to count the money to make sure it was all there. If it was, and everything checked out, they would release the hostages within fifteen days. Then they said goodbye and fled back into the jungle.

The clergy returned to the Ackerman group with the unwelcome news, and the wait began anew. Foreign Affairs officials in Ottawa worried the exhausting, protracted negotiations would prove to be all for naught. They worried the guerrillas might decide that if the company could hand over $3.5 million, it could surely afford more.

Gord Black received word in Vancouver that the ransom had been paid but the guerrillas hadn't honoured their part of the deal. He knew what would happen if the guerrillas reneged. There would be an enormous manhunt, and this time it wouldn't involve just the Ecuadorean military. Canadian and American authorities would move in with a vengeance. From his years of negotiating experience, he hoped the delay was just that—a delay. He hoped the guerrillas would let the hostages go, now they'd received their money. He hoped it was just a matter of time.

On December 12, three days after Barney's abortive escape attempt, Commandant, Vladimir and Old Tracker finally reappeared at the camp, carrying two military backpacks and a green nylon bag. They offered no explanation about where they'd been, or what their cargo was.

But the guerrillas' movements and actions around the bags made it obvious what was in them. From the moment the bags came into camp, a guerrilla loomed nearby and Michael and Goldstar made frequent trips to town for supplies, returning with piles of newspaper and packing tape. They needed to wrap something, and that something was cash, sitting in the backpacks and in the green nylon bag.

Sure enough, a couple of days later, in clear sight of the hostages, the guerrillas began pulling handfuls of bills out of the bags. They sifted through wads of crisp currency, separating the bills to ensure they hid no bugs, beacons or other tracking devices. Using tape and newspapers, they methodically stacked the cash in bundles, then wrapped several stacks to form thick bricks. Vladimir explained to Rod that they'd taken several days longer than expected to return from the drop-off point because the Ecuadorean army had surrounded them and forced them to hide until they could beat a safe retreat back to the camp.

For three more days, from dawn to dusk, Rod heard the sounds of stretching, snapping tape as the guerrillas worked through the money. He'd dreamed of the day United would hand over the ransom, thinking of the sweet relief. But now, as he watched the kidnappers methodically counting the bills, he wondered what the hell he and the other hostages were still doing there. *Why would United pay all this money and* not *get us out? Did United not demand our release as part of the deal?*

He spoke to Barney about his misgivings. "Isn't this odd?" Rod asked him. "In every movie you see, they never hand the money over until they get the hostages. It's always in the middle of a bridge somewhere. One group walks up with the money, another group walks up with the hostages, and they trade. They got their money, so why are we still here?"

Barney didn't need convincing. "Yeah, why go out of their way to get us to safety now that they got paid? We're toast now."

The guerrillas claimed they'd netted $1 million for each *gringo*—a cool $8 million for the three-month operation. The kidnappers were in such an ebullient mood, the hostages would have believed them if they said they received $100 million. They smiled all the time, and constantly play-wrestled each other around the camp. They no longer bothered to train their machine guns on the pipeliners. One guerrilla still guarded their tarpaulin shelter at night, but otherwise they hardly seemed to notice the hostages were there. The pipeliners could now go to the toilet in the bush without an armed escort and even ventured into the supply tent, though there was little there except for powdered cream, coffee and other dry foods.

Rod asked Chemaisu how much each guerrilla's take of the ransom would be. Chemaisu said he would make only $50,000, which he clearly considered a pittance. Chemaisu frequently talked about Harley-Davidson motorcycles, and often walked past the hostages' tent making engine-revving sounds. Rod asked him if he planned to purchase a Hog with his share of the ransom. Chemaisu shook his head. Most of the money would be used to purchase new machine guns, grenades and automatic pistols, he said.

Yeah, right. By the time we're back in Canada, you'll be on some tropical beach in the Caribbean sipping pina coladas for the rest of your life.

Rod asked if he and the hostages could see the money up close. He wanted to hold in his hands the reason he was here. The guerrillas agreed and marched the men three at a time to the money-wrapping station up a slight hill.

Grant, Colin and Rod walked up together. The guerrillas handed each man in turn a brick of money, which felt more like a cement block. There were unwrapped $100 U.S. bills in the military backpacks, stamped US Federal Reserve. They looked fresh from the mint. Rod marvelled at the money as he held it, at its sheer heft. He guessed the smaller stacks were $10,000 and the bigger brick at least $100,000. If so, it was a year's salary for him—three or four years' for some people. He handed it back to the guerrilla, shaking his head at his captors' greed and audacity. For a fleeting moment, he felt a grudging respect for what they'd pulled off.

The guerrilla then handed Colin the bundle of money and Colin turned his shoulders as if he were about to walk away with it. "Oh! *Gracias!*" he said with a laugh. The guerrillas laughed, too, but Colin didn't push his luck—he handed it back without taking a single step.

Later that afternoon, with the guerrillas still preoccupied with their money, the pipeliners nagged Barney to make them some coffee at the camp stove. But Barney wasn't in the mood; he was still troubled by the conversation he'd had with Rod about the guerrillas' reasons for failing to release them.

"Oh, come on, Barnz," said Rod. "Just go down there and make us some coffee. We're tired. We need a lift."

"No, I don't want coffee," Barney snapped back. "Why is it always me who has to do it? I'm not going. I'm not going this time."

Colin piped up: "OK, I'll make it. Just tell me where it is and I'll do it."

Barney barely looked up, but told Colin the stove didn't work properly, that he'd have to spray a little gasoline on the burner before he ignited it. Other than that, Barney said, it was just like lighting a regular camp stove.

A few minutes later, there was a dull thud, and the pipeliners looked up to see five-metre-high flames roaring out of the guerrillas' makeshift kitchen. Both the log table and the stove were fully engulfed. Black smoke billowed, and flames licked at the khaki-coloured tarp that hid the kitchen from the view of patrolling military helicopters.

Colin had been too generous in applying the gasoline from the spray bottle, managing to spill some on the stove, the ground and the log table the guerrillas used as a counter.

"Holy shit!" screamed Colin, hopping back and forth as if his feet were being stung by Congos. "Holy shit! I lit the kitchen on fire!"

Lario came running, machine gun in hand, and for a moment it looked like Colin was about to pay the ultimate price for his mistake. But when Lario saw the fire, he stopped dead in his tracks and doubled over laughing. Colin stared back at him, unsure whether to run or stay and help. Finally, Lario composed himself, ran inside the tent and pulled two propane tanks out of harm's way. Another guerrilla used the barrel of his gun to pull the tarp out of the flames.

Colin still stood there, clueless about what to do, unable to gauge how much trouble he was in.

"I, uh, I think I'm going to, um, get some water now," Colin said to Lario, matter-of-factly, then walked ten steps towards the stream as if nothing had happened. "I'm just, uh, going to run down here and get some water."

By now, all the hostages were laughing hysterically. If Colin had done that in the first week after they'd been taken, they'd all be dead! The sheer madness of it all made the pipeliners laugh even harder.

After the money came into the camp, the guerrillas even allowed the hostages to handle their weapons, once they'd unloaded the chambers, of course. Rod asked for Chemaisu's 9-mm Glock. He locked his elbows and pointed the barrel into the trees. After more than three months on the other side of the gun, Rod felt an odd flash of power as he cradled the Glock.

Chemaisu grinned and showed Rod a Colt .45 and a .38 Special. Rod asked if he could see Chemaisu's prized possession, a 9-mm Beretta. Chemaisu said no, but emptied the chamber of his gun. A hollow-point bullet fell into the dirt. The guerrilla picked it up and placed it in Rod's hand.

Rod felt a shiver run through him as he accepted the present. "This bullet means much more than a bullet," Rod said to Chemaisu. "This bullet could have killed me or any one of us."

Chemaisu patted his machine gun and smiled and Rod figured that the guerrilla understood that he knew all too well what the bullet represented. It was a telling exchange between the two men, and Rod knew he didn't have to fear Chemaisu any more.

Not long after Rod received his lethal souvenir, the guerrillas began to disappear one by one, as silently and stealthily as they'd appeared to the hostages in the gravel highway's dusty ditch three months before. They did not announce their departure, but simply vanished, like chastened spirits, into the jungle. Luki, the salsa-dancing, helicopter-shooting guerrilla, was the first, followed closely by the monstrous Muscles, pudgy Fabio, second-in-command Joto and the womanizer Michael. They left their packs, their hammocks, virtually everything they had, and slipped away. Rod thought they might come back, but they didn't.

Before he left, in the middle of a clear, cloudless day, Big Mac formed a pyre of camouflage jackets, pants and vests in front of the hostages' shelter and lit it on fire. Rod watched as Vladimir joined in, digging through the remaining guerrillas' backpacks and tossing in everything from underwear to hats to hammocks onto the blaze. Another guerrilla combed the kitchen for anything that could be disposed of, including a bag of rice, its sides flowering with green mould. Rope, tape, newspapers—all were fed to the hungry conflagration.

Black smoke billowed seven metres into the air, but none of the guerrillas seemed to notice, or care. The kidnappers felt unstoppable now they had their money. If the army came, the guerrillas would just abandon the hostages and cut through the trees to safety.

The atmosphere grew merry, almost celebratory. Rod asked Lario for the paper list that contained all the hostages' home

addresses and Lario just shrugged and handed it over. Rod cere-
moniously dumped it into the flames, then added his work coveralls and the putrid, stiff underwear he'd stopped wearing about
a month into the ordeal. His eyes stinging from the smoke, he
stared as the camp, piece by piece, burned away. The guerrillas
were clever—the authorities would be hard-pressed to track them
now their traces had been incinerated.

By now, most of the guerrillas had left, probably headed home
for Christmas, dressed as law-abiding, peace-loving civilians.
Rod guessed the fire was a signal that the end was near. *They
wouldn't burn all this stuff if they planned to move us to another
camp. Would they have the guts to fess up to their children about their
job, about the reason they had been gone for three months? Would
Luki make it home in time to trade his rubber boots for his dancing
shoes and take his wife to grand Christmas parties with his share of
the money?*

Lario was one of the last guerrillas to leave and strangely, Rod
had conflicted emotions about the clumsy guerrilla's impending
departure. Rod hated all the kidnappers for what they'd done,
with an intensity and a ferocious depth of which he never knew
he was capable. But he was grateful on some level that Lario had
tried to take care of the Canadians the best he could under the circumstances. On some level, Rod knew Lario cared; the guerrilla
had taken to apologizing profusely to the hostages for taking
them away from their families for so long. It was clear he'd been
wracked by guilt, and Rod knew that the drama and torment of
the abduction had deeply affected the gentle kidnapper equally as
much, in some ways, as it had affected him.

Lario spent much of his last day joking around and asking the
pipeliners about Christmas in snowy Canada. He produced
Barney's digital camera—the one the guerrillas had confiscated
on the day of their capture on the pipeline—and asked Barney
to show him how to use it. The two combed the bushes for

brilliantly coloured butterflies to capture on film. Rod teased Barney: "Isn't that sweet? Barney and Lario prancing through the jungle taking pictures of all the pretty butterflies." But Rod knew Lario was just delaying the inevitable, keeping his mind off the subject of leaving.

At 5 p.m., Lario returned from his photography excursion. He wandered teary-eyed about the camp, pouring rice and water into a pot, then placed it on the Coleman stove. Abruptly, he picked up his machine gun, grabbed some leftover tins of food from the supply tent, and disappeared into the thick brush, sparing nary a glance at the oil workers. His only farewell to the hostages was the rice—untended and quickly scorched—he left on the stove.

"That is so strange," Rod later said to Barney while they ate the rice. "He took the best care of us and he doesn't even say good-bye."

"Maybe it was too hard for him," said Barney.

The next morning, Rod awoke to a sharp tug on the rope of his hammock. He rubbed his eyes and looked up to see Commandant and Old Tracker hovering over him. It was still dark, but Rod saw that both guerrillas had shaved their beards— he almost didn't recognize them.

Old Tracker grabbed Rod's hand and shook it.

"Merry Christmas," Old Tracker said in perfect English. "Thank you."

"*Feliz Navidad,*" Commandant said, firmly shaking Rod's hand and staring him in the eyes. "You go *casa. Casa mañana.*"

Rod replied: "Thank you. Merry Christmas." As soon as it came out of his mouth, he wondered why he'd said it. *He stole my freedom, and now I'm thanking him. It doesn't make sense. Maybe it's true what they say about Canadians, that we're too polite.*

Later that morning, Rod awoke for a second time to find only Chemaisu and Vladimir remaining in the camp. Commandant, Old Tracker and the others had stolen away while he slept. The only things left in the camp, apart from the hostages' belongings and hammocks, were some empty tents, the Coleman stove, and four sets of leftover camouflage gear. Commandant had left behind the tiny transistor radio. Rod stuffed it in among his belongings as a souvenir. Neither Chemaisu nor Vladimir seemed to mind.

Vladimir told Rod that he, Chemaisu and the eight hostages would leave for Lago Agrio at noon. He pointed to his watch for emphasis.

Around 10 a.m., Rod heard three loud knocks on a nearby tree. He thought nothing of it, but watched as Vladimir picked up two sets of leftover camouflage gear and walked with them toward the source of the three knocks. Vladimir vanished from sight, returning a few minutes later without his camouflage gear. Rod felt his nerves give their familiar twang—he could sense something was about to happen.

Then, two men Rod had never seen before emerged from the thick trees and walked into the clearing outfitted head-to-toe in Vladimir's camouflage. They gripped automatic pistols tightly in their hands, their index fingers quivering on the hair-triggers. They, too, wore handkerchiefs with the message "Kill them all, let God sort them out," but pulled the cloths over their faces until nothing showed but their eyes.

What the fuck? thought Rod, before Barney intoned: "Oh, oh, here comes the clean-up crew. There's two of them now, but they'll get six more, then eight, then ten. We're done."

"Barnz, I'm warning you, buddy," said Rod. "Shut up!"

But Barney didn't. "They're coming in to kill us because the other guys grew too attached to us to do the dirty work," Barney said.

Rod didn't want to admit it, but he thought Barney was right. The nervous new guards looked shaky and meek compared to the confident, professional guerrillas. Maybe they were local farmers hired by the guerrillas to finish the job by killing the hostages and burning their bodies.

"Maybe you're right, maybe the guerrillas grew a bond with us. Maybe they just didn't have it in them to finish the job. Maybe they gave these guys a hundred bucks to come in and blow us away."

Vladimir and Chemaisu ordered the new guards to watch the oil workers as they themselves prepared to leave. The guards took their orders to heart, following the hostages' every move with their pistols.

"Five minutes with these guys and I'm already freaking out," Barney whispered. "They're going to kill us."

Another two clean-up crew members arrived at the camp that afternoon. Chemaisu gave them the other two sets of camouflage gear and two automatic pistols.

Noon passed and the men became impatient, nagging Chemaisu and Vladimir about when they would finally get to start out for Lago Agrio. They'd been promised so many times that their release was near, they feared this latest promise was a lie as well.

Chemaisu tried to keep the peace by agreeing to take a few pictures of the men with Barney's camera. Barney glared at Chemaisu, his old enemy, while the guerrilla snapped several pictures. Rod held Chemaisu's bullet in his hand and looked grimly at the camera. Assembled together, in their scruffy, dirty rags, the eight pipeliners looked like starving outdoorsmen returning from the hunting trip from hell.

Rod joked that Chemaisu and Vladimir should pose for a picture, but they refused.

Finally, at 3 p.m., Vladimir said *"Vamoose"* and the eight hostages, Vladimir and Chemaisu and the four clean-up crew members—fourteen men in all—marched away from the camp. The guerrillas left the Coleman stove and empty tents behind. Perhaps they'd arranged for some sympathetic local to fetch whatever they'd left behind.

Soon it started to pour—it figures, Rod thought miserably—and, drenched to the skin, the guerrillas, the clean-up crew and the hostages broke a trail through the jungle, ascending and descending steep hills, wading through swamps and climbing over rocks. Vladimir set a back-breaking pace, telling them they had to hurry because they were on a tight schedule. At times, the group broke into a jog through the trees.

It wasn't long before the hostages' worn bodies rebelled. Grant, who had developed horrible stomach problems, puked over and over, often in mid-stride. Barry soon fell behind.

Vladimir told Rod that a car had been arranged to take the men to Lago Agrio tomorrow. But if the hostages couldn't keep up the pace, they wouldn't be released for another two days because he'd need forty-eight hours to arrange another ride. Rod passed the message on to Barry and Grant, and the pair somehow managed to keep up.

After several hours, the group reached a stream at the bottom of a hill. Vladimir and Chemaisu handed out cigarettes to the pipeliners and spoke to the clean-up crew in stern tones, giving them orders about what to do next.

Vladimir then turned to the hostages. "You guys *vamoose* that way," he said pointing up the steep hill. "We *vamoose* this way. You go *casa mañana*."

Vladimir pointed to the number one on his watch. Tomorrow, the hostages would be released at a predetermined point in the jungle, and at one o'clock, they would hear three bangs on a tree—the signal that the car was ready to take them to Lago Agrio. He gave Rod 50,000 pesos, instructing him not to give the money to the clean-up crew, but to use it to pay the driver.

Vladimir then pointed at the four nervous, camouflaged clean-up crew members. "These guys, friends." Vladimir said. "Friends, friends, *no problemo*."

Rod nodded, and looked over at Chemaisu, who was staring back at him. Unbelievably, the guerrilla had tears in his eyes.

"Merry Christmas," he said, giving Rod a big bear hug. "Merry Christmas, friends." In fact, Chemaisu hugged all the men—

even Barney, whom he'd taunted regularly and almost killed over a bag of oats. He handed over two machetes to the hostages to break trail with, one to Neil and one to Steven. Then, as though they'd completed a simple business transaction, Vladimir and Chemaisu said "Thank you" and fled silently into the bush.

Rod handed the money to Barry, who tucked it into his shirt pocket and the hostages waited for the clean-up crew's next move. It came when the crew's apparent leader, a tall, lanky man, motioned to the hill, as if to ask whether the weary workers were prepared to continue the arduous trek.

"OK, guys, you ready to go?" Rod asked. A resounding chorus replied: "Yep, let's get this over with."

As he climbed the hill, Rod eyed the clean-up crew member directly in front of him. He was short and looked frail and Rod figured he could easily overpower him from behind, grab his gun and shoot the leader in the back of the head before anyone even noticed the insurrection. Hopefully, Neil and Skunk would follow his cue and chop the other two guards in half with their machetes.

But it was a fleeting thought. Rod conceded in his mind that there was no reason to take such drastic action now, when it appeared they were about to be finally freed.

The march took the men through farmers' fields, one bordered by a shiny, sharp new barbed-wire fence. Rod pushed down on the fence's top wire so the others could swing their weary legs over. As the last of the hostages clambered over, a staple popped out of the post and sliced into his hand.

"Shit!" he screamed, yanking his hand away as though he had been stung by wasps. The cut was thin, but deep. Blood was squirting from the wound, over his hand and down his arm. The pouring rain diluted the blood and spread the gore over his clothes. He looked like he'd been shot and stabbed.

The clean-up crew's lanky leader heard Rod's scream and dashed to the front of the group. The head guard saw Rod's wound and glared at the camouflaged men in front, berating them in Spanish. But the junior guards just shook their heads and put their hands in the air as if to say they'd done nothing wrong. One of the guards rushed to bandage Rod's hand with supplies from a first-aid kit. Though his wound was throbbing, Rod was almost happy the accident had happened—the clean-up crew's reaction indicated they were under orders to keep the hostages safe and healthy.

The group continued marching into the early evening hours. Rod was exhausted, he felt like his boots were filled with concrete. The hostages struggled up the fall line of a steep hill, gasping for air, leaning on fallen logs for support. Finally, the tall leader ordered the group to stop. "Carry on or *finito*?" he asked.

The men looked at one another. They couldn't take another step.

"*Finito*," said Rod. "We're *finito*."

The guards borrowed the two machetes from Neil and Steven to cut down trees to hang the tarps on. Rod lay on the soaking ground and tried to close his eyes to sleep. He tossed and turned, and could hear that the other men were restless, too.

Is the freedom we've lived for almost within reach, or are the rank amateurs in the clean-up crew going to fuck everything up?

After so many days of dreaming, wishing and praying for our release, is it finally going to happen?

Cold Cervesas

THE RAIN FINALLY STOPPED, but the men woke at dawn on December 19 drenched to the bone, soaked blankets clinging to their clammy, cold skin. They'd hardly slept.

Would today be the day? Rod wondered.

The clean-up crew roused the men and told them to get going. Steven and Neil asked for their machetes back, but the nervous guards said no, not yet. Rod figured they had probably grown uncomfortable about allowing the hostages the means to chop off their heads.

The guard in front again set a lightning-quick pace, striding through the jungle, elbowing obstacles out of the way. Rod, judging from his haste, thought they had a long trek ahead of them before meeting the car at 1 p.m.

The morning's warmth dried the men's stiff clothes as they marched through the trees. The group stopped only occasionally, to let Grant catch up after he threw up or dropped his pants in the trees, crippled by diarrhea cramps.

At about 10 a.m., after nearly four hours of non-stop hiking up treacherous inclines and down steep declines, the group approached a coffee field. The United workers were ordered to sit. Farmers on horses and child pickers walked through the field, giving the hostages and their armed guards a wide berth. They stared at the grimy *gringos* as if they were some bizarre, exotic animals they'd never seen before.

The clean-up crew's leader disappeared for about an hour, then returned with a pack of cigarettes and some lemons he'd picked from a nearby tree. He looked nervously down at his watch. It was 11 a.m.

Struggling to communicate with Rod in Spanish, the leader mimicked what Vladimir had told him: the hostages were to walk to a nearby river, which they could see through the trees, and follow along it until they came to a bridge. After traversing the bridge, they were to wait until 1 p.m., when they would hear three knocks on a tree. A car would then arrive to take them to Lago Agrio.

The crew members, relief flooding their faces, said, "Thank you," and pumped the hostages' hands. Rod returned the gesture with equal enthusiasm. He felt no anger towards the crew. They were mere accessories to the guerrillas' crime, poor, peasant farmers lured by the promise of big money to return the hostages to civilization. They were obviously out of their league, terrified, and apart from their itchy trigger fingers, had no intention of doing the hostages harm. Rod, in a charitable moment, hoped the money they earned from the guerrillas would give their families a better Christmas.

The clean-up crew handed the machetes back to Neil and Steven, turned on their heels and disappeared into the jungle, like puffs of smoke.

It was an odd moment. The men stood, finally out of the clutch of armed men, with explicit directions to freedom. Still, Rod didn't feel free. He did not feel like pausing to celebrate. He did not feel like waiting around for some car. He felt like getting the hell out of there.

Rod led the group down a muddy path beside the river, continuing to feel like the group was still in danger. From what parties or forces, he did not know, but his uneasiness remained as strong as when he was still held captive.

He looked over his shoulder and was struck by how awful everyone looked, how the other men were nearing their limits. Barney hobbled on his bum ankle, wincing and grunting with every step. Grant was sheet-white and nearly staggering. Barry, bearded and haggard, looked ready to pass out at any moment from heat exhaustion. But their eyes were stern and focused; they would keep walking until they died.

Rod spied the bridge, crossed the river, and the jungle opened up a bit. He immediately spotted a farmhouse on top of the hill. To his right lay a heavily beaten path, to his left, a less frequently used path appeared to lead to the farmhouse. Rod caught his breath as he waited for the rag-tag group of co-workers to catch up.

Once assembled, the men argued about what to do next. Two or three thought they should take the less-travelled path towards the farmhouse. Others thought they should take the beaten trail, reasoning that it might lead to Lago Agrio. Still others contended they should stay put and wait for the car as they'd been ordered, worried they might somehow still pay dearly for defying the guerrillas.

It may have been reckless, but Rod said there was no way he was waiting for the car, out in the open like a sitting duck.

"We're fucking out of here," he said. "We're not waiting for any truck. This looks like a heavily used trail. We'll stick to it until we get to a road and then hire a cab. We'll walk for half an hour. We can turn around if it looks like it doesn't lead anywhere. That way we'll be back in time for this car. But we're not sitting still."

They walked for that half an hour down the muddy trail, then stopped in front of another farmhouse. They stood, panting, and the argument about what to do next flared again.

"Well, what the hell are we doing?" said Colin. "What's our plan? Do we have a plan?"

Barry weighed in: "We're walking down this path. It's better than sitting and doing nothing. Who knows if there's ever going to be a car? Do you want to sit and wait forever or wait until more guerrillas find us and drag us right back into the bush? Do you have a better plan?"

Colin snapped back at him: "This is a fine time for you to be showing some leadership, Barry. You weren't much of a fucking leader when we were in the jungle."

The argument boiled nearly to the point of flying fists, when Barry backed down.

"I know, I know," he said, looking tired and old. "I know I haven't been the best role model. Whatever you guys say. Majority rules."

Finally Rod said: "OK, I want one guy to come with me. We'll walk to this house and ask if this trail goes to Lago Agrio."

Colin agreed to join him, and the two men started up the path until Rod saw four women staring at them from the sad little farmhouse's dilapidated front room. Rod made eye contact with one of the women, and they all scurried away.

Great. What do we do now? No wonder they're scared of us. We're filthy, we're shouting at one another, we're lost.

Before any of them could move, Rod heard the clip-clop of hooves. Two dark-skinned young farmers in shorts and T-shirts came ambling down the path, leading a donkey and carrying propane tanks in their hands.

"Skunk, take out your machete," Rod hissed, but both Steven and Neil had already instinctively drawn their weapons. They wanted to let the strangers know they were armed.

Rod had no time for niceties. He approached the farmers and said: "This trail, Lago Agrio? Lago Agrio?"

"*Si, si,* Lago Agrio," one of them replied.

"Please help. Guerrillas stole us," said Barney, making machine-gun noises. "*Gringos. Casa* Canada."

The farmer started speaking excitedly in Spanish, but all Rod could catch were the words "Maria" and "Canada." It hit him like a thunderbolt—this was the same man who'd found Maria, Jesus and Sabine!

Rod hoped that the farmer was friendly, that finding Maria hadn't caused him any problems. He asked, "You, you? You go to Lago Agrio?" The farmer nodded: "*Si, si.* Lago Agrio. *No problemo.*" He waved his hand at Rod, beckoning him to follow.

The men hustled along the trail behind the two farmers and their donkey. They hoisted Grant on the donkey's back to give him a chance to rest. Rod worried Grant might collapse at any moment—his face was drained of colour, and looked especially pale against his shaggy, dark beard. Grant had hiked mile after mile through his pain, dizziness and nausea.

As they moved closer to civilization, locals appeared on the roadside, giving the hostages large, fleshy, sweet grapes to eat. Rod asked the farmer when they would arrive in Lago. The farmer pointed at the three on his watch. Another two hours.

After another hour, the farmers led the men into a rainforest hamlet. Rod's eyes immediately locked on a small cantina on the side of the hamlet's main dirt road. Through the dusty window, he swore he could see the glimmer of beer bottles stacked neatly on a shelf.

Rod looked at the farmer. "*Cervesas, cervesas?*"

The farmer shook his head, motioning for the group to keep walking down the road. They turned a corner and the farmer pointed excitedly at a ramshackle house that doubled as a bar.

"*Cervesas,*" the farmer said. "Cold *cervesas.*"

Rod laughed out loud, and the other hostages—even poor, sick Grant—whooped. The farmer obviously knew that the beer wasn't as frosty at the cantina Rod had spotted.

The hostages, covered head to toe in filth, reeking worse than a football locker room, entered the bar, pulled up eight chairs and ordered several rounds. It was there, in the dimly lit bar, that the enormity of the moment hit them.

After 100 days in the jungle, they were finally free.

As the bartender brought them their cold brews, many of the

men broke down, forcing out with every hitched sob the terror and pressure of the past 100 days. There were bear hugs and spirited high-fives all around.

"Hey, we're out man. We did it. We made it," Rod cried out, sitting at a table with Barney, his old friend, and Barry, the man with whom he'd had so many conflicts in the jungle. Rod and Barry grinned widely and shook hands. Where there were once hard feelings, Rod now felt a bond with Barry—with all of the men—that could not be broken. In the jungle, they'd stared sickness, horror and death in the eyes, and had not blinked.

"No matter what happens now, Barry, no matter who comes out of that bush, we ain't going back!" said Rod. Barry smiled and nodded. "Fucking right," he said.

Barney smiled a true, broad grin, the kind Rod remembered seeing back in Canada. "I'd sell my house for this beer!" Barney whooped.

By this time, dozens of curious village children gathered around the bar, staring curiously at the soiled *gringos*. Barney, like a magician, produced a wad of American money—he'd had it stashed away in a leather pouch the entire time in the jungle, hidden away from the guerrillas' sight. Barney bought Fanta pops for the entire gaggle of kids, then picked up sixteen beers for the road and enough crackers, buns and chocolate for a week.

But when even more locals arrived, the men began to feel uneasy about the attention they were attracting.

"I feel like I'm in a petting zoo," Barney told Rod. "We're safe, but we're not safe. Let's get out of here."

Rod led the men out of the bar and across the street, where they spotted a truck. After a few seconds of quick negotiations, Rod convinced the driver to haul them to Lago Agrio for $5 a head. The pipeliners hopped into the truck's box and the vehicle tore down the road. The men downed beers along the way, tossing empty cans into the ditch, erupting in cheers and toasts when

Rod spotted a pipeline next to the road. The smooth, round steel was like a totem, a signpost—it meant Lago Agrio was near.

Suddenly, the men lurched forward when the truck slammed on its brakes, skidding in the gravel. Rod looked out over the cab and saw several Ecuadorean soldiers in fatigues. "Hide the beer! Hide the beer!" he yelled to his friends. After three months of enduring inhuman jungle conditions at the hands of armed terrorists, they were all still good Canadian boys at heart, worried about receiving a ticket for having open liquor in a vehicle.

An Ecuadorean army private approached the truck. He asked the pipeliners for documents. Rod shrugged and could only think to say: "*Ochos gringos*"—eight foreigners. One of the pipeliners standing behind Rod uttered the word "kidnapped."

That was all it took. Suddenly, four soldiers stepped to the truck, shouldering enormous .50-calibre machine guns. The soldiers hustled the men out of the truck, lined them up along the side of the road, and switched bigger ammunition clips into their guns.

Rod, understandably wary of anyone wearing camouflage, wondered if this perhaps wasn't, in fact, the cavalry.

"This is not good," whispered Barney. "They're going to shoot us. This is it!"

Rod shared Barney's fears. *Maybe these are corrupt soldiers on the payroll of some other guerrilla group, or legitimate military, angry they didn't find us on their own.* In the wilds of Ecuador, there was no telling who to trust, especially if they wore green fatigues.

Just then a plain-clothes officer skidded up to the scene in a truck. He stepped from the cab barking into a cell phone and immediately ordered the hostages to jump into the box of his truck. A machine-gun-toting soldier crouched beside them, his finger on the trigger, the safety off and the chamber full. As the truck spun out of the gravel and flew down the road, the pipeliners found themselves in the middle of a vast convoy of army vehicles. Every few hundred metres, other vehicles would appear from a jungle side road and join at either the front or back of the line. As the convoy grew, so did the men's confidence.

"Holy shit, I bet the president doesn't get this much protection," Rod said to Barney. He paused, looked down to the floor of the truck's box, and thrust his chin at the soldier. "We still have a few beers left. Do you think he'll mind?"

"No," Barney said, gleefully. "Go for it!"

Rod even offered the soldier a beer, but the private sternly shook his head. Rod then reached into the bag of chocolates and offered a few to the army man, who smiled and ate some of the candies. The truck roared on, finally hitting pavement. On the horizon, the men could see the refineries and smokestacks, and knew it was Lago Agrio.

The United workers were spirited to the oil town's army base, where they gave a brief account of their time with the kidnappers. Allied Intelligence security men had already assembled at the base, and rushed the hostages to the makeshift safe house they'd set up at a heavily guarded resort hotel. The word "resort" in the hotel's name implied splendour, though that was hardly the case. But the men didn't care. It was far more comfortable than the hard, insect-infested jungle floor.

The pipeliners were ordered to hand over anything they'd brought out of the jungle so the authorities could scan the items for clues. Rod reluctantly handed over his bullet—the hard-won souvenir and symbol of his survival—but managed to sneak the guerrillas' transistor radio back to his hotel room by stuffing it in his rubber boot. Barney complied when asked to give them his digital camera and his prized diskette. Steven and Neil passed the soldiers their machetes.

Heaven, in the form of clean clothes and their first hot shower in 100 days, awaited in their rooms. Allied purchased new track suits, underwear and shoes for the men. Shaving kits sat on their beds.

Rod showered, revelling in the clean, clear water, the abundance of soap and shampoo, the luxury of fresh towels. When he got out of the shower, he picked up his old sweat pants and T-shirt from the floor and threw them into the garbage, trying not to gag from the smell.

The men assembled in one of the hotel's spartan conference rooms, and were examined by a team of doctors who prescribed several kinds of pills for each. Barney's ankle finally received attention, and Rod asked the physicians to look at the hip he pulled dragging Barney through the jungle.

Michael Intravia, a private investigator from Allied Intelligence, produced five cell phones, announcing that the men were free to call their families and talk for as long as they wished.

Rod broke down as soon as he heard Jane's voice. For the first time since Krissy was born, he cried.

"I'm here. I'm out. I'm OK," he said, his voice wracked, his throat choked with emotion. "I'll be home soon. I love you. I love you."

"Oh my God, Rod," she said. "I don't know what to say."

"I know," he said. "I know."

They cried for two minutes, barely managing to utter a coherent word. Rod could hear Krissy yelling in the background, "Let me talk to Daddy!"

Jane let their daughter on the line. "Hi Daddy," Krissy said. "I love you. Are you coming home now?"

"I'll be there soon, Tweet," he said. "Just a few more days, and I'll be home. I love you."

Rod hung up the phone and sobbed.

━━━━━━━━

Canadian officials reacted with glee to the news the hostages had been released. Gar Pardy and Helen Harris, the Foreign Affairs officials who had worked on the case since the men were captured, shared a bottle of red wine—good red wine—in Pardy's Ottawa office. Gord Black, who had just arrived in Quito the day before on December 18 to relieve John Tost, flew immediately to Lago Agrio after the men had been freed. With the negotiations over, his job now was to make sure the men returned home safely to Canada.

In Lago Agrio, the Mountie rushed to the resort where the Ecuadorean army had quarantined the freed hostages. Gord saw the twenty-five-wide column of soldiers standing guard against the wall bordering the resort property, along with the several men patrolling the grounds within, and knew the hostages faced no danger.

Inside the resort's gates, Gord met his fellow negotiators, FBI agents Dennis Braiden and George Kazynski, and his peers from UNASE, the elite Ecuadorean police anti-kidnap squad. The reunion was joyous. Dennis and George pointed to the room where the freed hostages were being protected, and Gord stepped through the door, chatting with the FBI men about the details of the hostages' release.

Gord, who'd spent hours memorizing the pictures of the Canadians from their driver's licences and photographs from home, instantly recognized Rod Dunbar and Grant Rankin. Grant, sitting in a swivel chair, wheeled around, pointed at Gord, and said, "I hear a Canadian voice!" Rod stood up and walked towards him.

"Hi guys," Gord said softly. "I'm an RCMP officer and I'm here to take you home."

Any remnants of his tough police demeanour slipped away, and Gord began to cry as he embraced the men, men he'd never met but had worked so hard to free. As a Mountie, he'd experienced first-hand the horrors of human tragedy many times— other kidnappings, murders. But here he was, witness finally to a tale with a happy ending, one he'd helped write. The men were going home.

Gord wiped his eyes and surveyed the group. Given their ordeal, he thought they looked remarkably well—pale and gaunt, but certainly not in critical condition. The hostages told him about the food they'd been forced to eat, the marches they'd endured, the insect swarms and the crotch rot.

The freed Canadians fired questions at Gord. What had happened in Canada while they were gone? Who won the Grey Cup? Had their kidnapping been in the news?

Gord answered all their questions patiently. Yes, they were on the front pages of newspapers and at the top of news broadcasts across the country. The Hamilton Tiger-Cats had won the Grey Cup.

Then he looked at the men and asked a question of his own: "What was the first thing you guys did when you walked out of the bush?"

The hostages looked at each other, reluctant to tell the truth. Finally, Rod shrugged and simply told the truth about the revelry at the ramshackle cantina.

Gord looked at Intravia, pounded his hand on the table and said, "See, I told you. You owe me twenty dollars." Gord had made Intravia a bet, and had won.

"Canadian boys," Gord said. "The first thing they'll do is go for beers."

Intravia and the other Allied people arranged for a homecoming feast for the freed pipeliners: They had prime rib, roast chicken, roast potatoes, salad, rice—good rice, not rice burned midnight black on an open flame. But after only a few bites, Rod was full. He couldn't eat another forkful. His stomach had shrunk in the jungle adapting to the meagre portions given to him by the guerrillas.

"I want to eat more, but I can't," he said.

"Don't eat to the point you get sick," Gord told them. "There's food here whenever you want. Don't push it."

After dinner, the Ecuadorean army drove the pipeliners back to the army base for interviews with the military and police. Gord escorted the group to make sure they were treated fairly and that the process didn't go on all night. At the base, the army passed out questionnaires asking the men's names, ages, and nationalities. They wanted to know whether they'd seen the guerrillas before the kidnapping and whether they could accurately describe the guerrillas to a graphic artist.

Rod didn't mind the queries, but was offended by a follow-up question: Did he or any of his family members in Canada have a criminal record? *Come on! Do you guys think we're guerrilla sympathizers who asked to be kidnapped?*

As the questioning dragged into the evening, the men became tired and frustrated. Gord assured them he wouldn't let the military interrogate them all night long. United made it clear the company wanted the men home for Christmas, Gord said. The top priority was to get the men on their way back to Canada to happy reunions with their families.

The men took turns giving their official statements to a UNASE officer and a military officer. A translator tapped the depositions into a computer. The ex-hostages described their 100-day nightmare from beginning to end. No detail was considered insignificant in the manhunt for the kidnappers.

The oil workers had plenty to tell. By midnight, only a few—Barry, Leonard, Colin—had made their statements. Finally, Gord saw the dark shadows around their weary eyes and cut the interviews short. He told his UNASE friends they were welcome to come to Edmonton after Christmas to interview the remaining four who signed a form, stating they would adopt the statements of their fellow hostages. The UNASE men seemed satisfied and ordered a military convoy to escort the men back to the hotel.

Rod, Grant and Barney were the last to retire for the night. Too excited to sleep, they stayed up with Gord relating more horror stories about life in the jungle. Rod spoke about the sicknesses and the alternating periods of boredom and terror when the men feared they would be shot. He talked about the frustrations of living side-by-side in captivity with seven co-workers, and about the guerrillas—Lario's klutzy ways, Commandant's no-nonsense manner, Chemaisu's temper tantrums and his surprising show of emotion just two days before their release.

Gord listened intently. He told the hostages they should be proud of their strength and determination. Lesser men would have given up and tried to escape, or would have been too exhausted to take another step.

"I can't imagine the hell you guys went through," Gord said. "I don't think anyone can."

"It was unbelievable," Rod said. "Are we going to get home soon?"

"Yeah, I'm staying with you the whole way," Gord promised. "We're going to get you to Edmonton."

At the word "Edmonton," everyone went quiet. This wasn't a lie, this wasn't one of the guerrillas saying "you go *casa, mañana.*" This was a Mountie talking about Edmonton, about home.

This was the truth.

At 5 a.m. on December 20, Gord, the freed pipeliners and the City Investing security men flew from Lago Agrio to Quito. In Ecuador's capital, Allied had arranged a military escort right from the tarmac to the Swissotel, a five-star downtown hotel, so the men would remain out of the prying sight of the hundreds of reporters and cameramen staking out the airport's entrance. Gord was pleased with the arrangements, marvelling at how efficient and professional Allied had been so far.

But after landing, under directions from air traffic control, the pilot taxied the plane away from the airport's commercial flight terminal building to the adjacent military base. Gord couldn't believe his eyes when he looked out the window to see a military receiving line—including Ecuador's highest-ranking general—setting up outside the plane. Knowing the freed hostages would not be game for any prolonged pomp and circumstance, Gord hurried down the plane's stairs to investigate.

An army officer explained that the men were to be re-interviewed by the military general. The interview would be videotaped, as would the "official" handing over of the oil workers to the "custody" of the RCMP. Gord didn't argue; he thought back to the scene in Lago Agrio when he rescued Sabine Roblain and remembered how touchy and possessive the Ecuadorean military could be.

Gord climbed back on to the plane and explained the situation to the hostages. "I know you guys aren't in the mood for this, but we can't insult our hosts," he said. "Just go inside the base and listen to what they have to say. You're going to be officially welcomed by the general and while he's talking, I'm going to talk to the ambassador and find out how to handle this situation."

The oil workers dutifully descended the stairs and shook the general's hand. They chatted with the general about their ordeal while Gord raised Ambassador John Kneale on a cell phone.

"Listen, Gord," Kneale said. "You are my direct representative. On behalf of the Government of Canada, go to the general and tell him we would prefer that this be done at a different location. Tell him the Canadian government will set up a reception for him and anyone he wants to bring along at the hotel. That will give him the exposure he needs."

Both Gord and Kneale recognized the need for the Ecuadorean army to take credit for the rescue of the men. Their reputation had been badly damaged by what the Ecuadorean public had overwhelmingly deemed a botched search effort. Tourists and foreign companies had lost confidence in Ecuador because of the hostage-taking. Complicating the country's situation was a currency crisis and the streets were alive with citizens enraged by the devalued *sucre*. Gord and Kneale decided that, given the situation, throwing the Ecuadoreans a free publicity bone was the least they could do.

Gord told the general he could have a brief interview with the hostages that could be recorded for their purposes. But any further discussions would have to take place at the hotel, after the Canadians were settled. The general agreed, and the weary hostages were quickly whisked away from the airport to their luxury quarters at the Swissotel, where Allied Intelligence had secured the entire fifth floor. An American tropical disease specialist, along with another team of doctors, awaited the group. They checked the hostages' vital signs repeatedly and did blood work to determine if they'd picked up any parasites in the jungle. Skunk had his head shaved for wood ticks, and the doctors tended to Leonard's toes. A beautician shaved the hostages' scraggly beards. Barney got the deluxe treatment, asking the woman for a manicure/pedicure and to dye his hair blond.

Food and beer arrived at the hotel all day—pizza, hamburgers, Kentucky Fried Chicken, french fries—and the men did their best to eat it all. Allied also managed somehow to ship in Canadian beer for the boys. Most of the men, especially Grant, were feeling better, although Barney took a turn for the worse. The elevation difference between Quito and Lago Agrio, combined with the excitement of going home, made Barney's asthma even worse than it had been in the jungle. The doctors also worried about the severity of his crotch rot.

"I'm scared they won't let me out of here," Barney told Rod. "The doctors say they want me to go to the hospital. That means you guys may go home without me."

"Don't worry, Barnz," said Rod. "You'd have to be dying for them to put you in the hospital. You're coming home with us."

"Nothing's going to stop me from being on that plane," Barney said defiantly.

That night, the Ecuadorean general and several other high-ranking officers attended a banquet at the Swissôtel. United managers Ken Foster and Rob Mackie flew in from Edmonton for the reunion. They all raised their glasses during a gracious toast Neil gave to Edison Jacome, the soldier who'd been killed on the pipeline. Neil spoke eloquently about how he had become friends with Edison despite their language barrier, and told of the horror and heartbreak he felt emerging from the fusion tent to find Edison's body riddled with bullets.

The general told the men he was deeply sorry about their ordeal. He promised the military and police would do everything they could to bring the guerrillas to justice and to ensure foreign workers never went through a similar ordeal again in Ecuador. He assured them that Ecuador valued the investment of North American oil companies. Without them, he insisted, the already shaky economy would crash even further—a concept guerrillas of any political stripe had failed to grasp.

Flash bulbs went off. Ecuadorean army and police officers shook the hostages' hands repeatedly. It was a regal affair.

Late that night, Barney received medical clearance to fly home and at 5 a.m. the next morning, the freed pipeliners, along with Foster, Mackie and Gord boarded a luxurious Gulfstream jet for the long flight back to Edmonton. Despite the early hour, the men cracked open fresh beers while they sat on the tarmac awaiting takeoff.

As the plane roared down the runway and lifted off, the men's spirits soared. A few minutes in, Gord announced that the plane had left Ecuadorean airspace, and the ex-hostages whooped and clinked bottles. Rod looked out the window, down on the jungle canopy bordering Ecuador and Colombia. "Can anyone see Luki down there?" he said. "I bet you he's trying to shoot us out of the sky with his machine gun."

The plane touched down in Panama City for more fuel and more beer. Rod enjoyed a cigarette under the plane's wing, keeping an eye on the armed soldiers who lined the tarmac. He couldn't wait to get back to Canada, where machine guns were the rare exception, not the rule.

The plane landed in Tucson to clear American customs, then flew the short hop to Phoenix to let Leonard off. Rod watched, a little jealously, as Leonard walked into a cordoned-off hangar and was soon mobbed by his jubilant family.

Leonard introduced the seven Canadians to his family and he and Rod swapped phone numbers, promising to keep in touch. The men reboarded the plane once again, and the men were quiet, visibly affected by Leonard's reunion. "That's going to be us in a few hours," said Skunk—quiet, withdrawn Skunk, who'd barely spoken during his time in the jungle. "That's going to be us."

Along with a new supply of beer, a gorgeous, brown-haired flight attendant came on board. Apart from Mrs. Tiger Tooth, she was the first woman the men had seen in more than three months.

Gord gave the attendant a good-natured warning. "These guys have been in the jungle for 100 days," he said. "You may want to remain scarce." She did, staying at the back of the plane, except to serve the men food or more beer.

About two hours later, the pipeliners erupted in cheers once again when Gord announced the plane had hit Canadian airspace. But the celebration died down as the men realized they'd see their families within the hour. Rod felt flushed with nervousness. *What will my family say when they see me? How are they going to react? For that matter, how am I going to react?*

As the plane passed over Calgary and zoomed north towards Edmonton the pilot dimmed the cabin lights. "Finish your drinks," he said. "We can see the lights of Edmonton now. You're almost home."

The plane landed at Edmonton's City Centre Airport, just

northwest of the city's downtown. As the plane taxied and came to a stop, the men could see two huge groups of people gathered in front of the hangar—the families on one side, the media on the other. Foster explained to the men that a special hangar was reserved for the men where they could reunite with their families in privacy. None of the men would have to speak to reporters.

Even so, there was still one more step. A customs official marched on to the plane and said, "I take it you have nothing to declare," as she inspected the men's passports.

"No!" screamed Barney. "Let us out! Throw down the stairs. Let's go!"

The men bounded off the plane to an explosion of cheers from the family members, who stood behind a barricaded area. Rod walked shoulder-to-shoulder with Barney, Grant, Colin and Neil.

He scanned the crowd for familiar faces and his heart leapt to this throat when heard Krissy's voice above the din: "Daddy, Daddy! You're home!" She ducked under the barricades and ran towards him, the first family member to reach the hostages.

Rod laughed as he leaned down to pick up his daughter. He had lost so much strength, he could barely lift her. "Krissy, I love you," he said, hugging her tightly.

When he looked up he saw his mom, his sisters, everyone. They were all crying. He felt a tap on his shoulder, turned and saw Jane, quietly sobbing.

"Your wife really needs a hug, Rod," she said. With Krissy still in his arms, he embraced his wife, and the three stood, huddling and crying in the mid-December chill.

"We made it," Rod said softly, wiping the tears from his wife's cheeks.

"We made it. That's all that matters."

Inside the hangar, the families milled about, hugging one another, yet seemingly drained by all the emotion. Gord wandered through the crowd, meeting the families of the men he'd helped rescue. An older man put his hand on the Mountie's shoulder. In a hoarse voice, he managed to say, "Thank you so much for bringing my boy home," then broke down in tears.

Gord was crying himself, looking at this man and the pure joy he felt to have his son back safe and sound. He reflected on the countless hours of work put in by the FBI, UNASE, the Ecuadorean military, the Canadian consular group.

I'm a lucky man, he thought. They think I'm the guy who went down to Ecuador and brought their boys and husbands back. But it was a team effort.

Rod approached Gord with his mother, Krissy and Jane at his side. Rod introduced his family and Gord told Rod's mother she should be proud of her son. Without his determination to learn to communicate with the guerrillas, he said, the men might not have pulled through. And without Rod's emotional and physical strength, Barney might very well have died in the jungle.

Rod told Gord that the Mountie was the one his mother should be proud of.

"As long as I live," Rod said to Gord, "I can never thank you or repay you enough for what you did."

The men hugged briefly, then Rod turned and walked away.

After 100 days of holding himself together, he was about to fall apart.

Aftermath

FROM THE HANGAR, after the hostages clutched each other a final time, Rod, Jane and Krissy drove home. The snowy streets and Christmas lights hung from the eaves of Edmonton's homes seemed magical, illusory. He could hardly believe his return was real, that he really was home.

On the flight from Quito, Rod had wondered how Jane would react, if she would regard him strangely or treat him as if he were a fragile object about to break. But driving home, he realized he had nothing to worry about. Although Jane had gone through her own private hell while he was in the hands of the guerrillas—she'd shed nearly twenty-five pounds from her petite frame—she seemed content now, overjoyed to have him home.

Rod sucked in his breath when he turned the corner onto his west Edmonton crescent, and let out a little cheer when he spotted his house. Rod was barely through the door before Krissy grabbed his hand and dragged him down to the basement.

"Daddy, we waited for you," she said shyly. "We waited until you got home to put the angel on."

Rod's eyes welled with tears. *God, I can't stop crying tonight.* Krissy held the angel in her hands as Rod, using all his waning strength, hoisted her up over his head to place the angel on top of the tree.

"Thank you, Daddy," Krissy said, and gave Rod a kiss on the cheek. She was delighted but serene, a seven-year-old girl excited about Christmas.

That night in bed, Jane held onto Rod. She was afraid he might disappear if she let go. He told her she could hold on as tight as she wanted.

The following day, United scheduled a news conference to give the men a chance to tell their story to the world. But Rod told his bosses he didn't want to talk. He felt weak and disoriented from the hostages' head-spinning retreat from Ecuador. Many of the other men agreed. Couldn't United just tell the media to fuck off?

But Ken Foster explained that if the freed hostages didn't speak out in a formal setting, reporters would hound them day and night over the Christmas holidays until they *did* speak. The phone would ring at all hours and television crews would camp out in front of their houses. This way they could talk to the media once, and then ask to be left alone over the holidays.

The United workers discussed the message they wanted to send to the world. No one among them would be labelled a hero. They would emphasize how remembering their families and helping each other had got them through the ordeal.

The news conference was to be held at the Holiday Inn, the same place where United had held the family meetings. The media loaded their cameras, microphones, lights and tape-recorders into the banquet room, all of them pointed to a long table at the front of the room where Foster and the seven pipeliners sat. Folding chairs were placed on either side of the table for family members willing to talk.

For the media, it was a huge story. They'd waited 100 days with hardly a glimpse into the lives of these seven ordinary Edmontonians thrown into such extraordinary circumstances.

Just before two, the family members, who'd kept a silent vigil for the past three months, hesitantly answered journalists' questions about how they felt when the pipeliners returned. They spoke in soft tones about the pain of not knowing the hostages' fate for so long, and the jubilation of having their sons and husbands back safe in Edmonton for Christmas.

Then, without fanfare, the hostages walked in, one by one. The families broke into cheers and applause. Colin gave a shy wave as the men took their seats. Barney and Rod sat side by side. Barney told Rod he could hardly keep his eyes open—he'd been drinking late into the night with family and friends at his old haunt, an Edmonton pub called Billy Budd's. He'd had a few beers, listened to music—rock music, not salsa—on the jukebox, shot some pool and regaled his friends with the hostages' unbelievable stories. Rod told Barney about his relatively quiet night, and talked about how nervous he was. His hands shook as he poured himself a glass of ice water and waited for the journalists' questions.

Foster told the reporters he would stop the news conference if he thought questions became too personal or intrusive. Then the queries began: "What did you eat?" "How did the guerrillas treat you?" "How did you survive it?" True to form, Skunk hardly said a word. Barry kept mostly quiet, and Rod, apart from hinting at the horror of his sickness early in the ordeal, fielded few questions. Colin, Neil, Barney and Grant did most of the talking, crediting all the hostages for making endurable the rotten food, the endless bouts of diarrhea, the insect bites and the fear of never seeing their loved ones again.

"Every day we talked about our families," said Colin. "Some days, there were good days, stories and jokes. Other days, we broke down.

"There are six guys here sitting at this table who got me out. We stuck together as a group and that's how we got out.

"I don't think I could have made it if I was alone. Every guy had a bad day, bad days where one guy would say, 'I'm gone. I'm running.' For us, as Canadians, our experience would have been Rambo movies and stuff like that, and those never turn out so good.

"Everybody had to stick together."

Barney said he owed his life to Rod for hauling him down to the creek the day his temperature spiked as he lay vomiting in his hammock.

"Rod kicked my ass out of bed one morning and said, 'We have to get you down to the creek to cool you off,'" he said. "It was the scariest feeling ever. When I was sick, I didn't think I was going to make 'er."

Grant said he almost collapsed from exhaustion the same night Barney injured his ankle.

"We just pushed each other to keep going, to keep alive and survive," he said. "It didn't matter to us why. We did whatever they wanted and co-operated, because we wanted to come home and see our families."

Colin talked about how the experience deepened his faith in God. He promised to attend church more from now on. And he talked about how facing death around the clock for 100 days changed his outlook on life.

"We were fairly critical of ourselves at times," he said. "We went there because it was a job for a company we work for, and I should have stayed home with my family.

"When you're just a couple months away from them, you see how much they grow and change."

For two hours, the hostages fielded questions from reporters, brushing off inquiries about the ransom or whether United had provided for enough security on the pipeline. They repeated Rod's first words upon arriving back in Edmonton: They were out. That's all that mattered.

Rod and Jane decided to spend a quiet Christmas with family and friends, abandoning Rod's idea to take a trip to Vegas. Now that he was finally home, travelling was the last thing he wanted to do. Besides, his mother and sisters would be devastated if he left immediately after being away for so long and under such harrowing circumstances.

Rod rushed around Christmas Eve to buy all his presents and, true to his jungle word, Rod bought Jane a deluxe built-in vacuum system and a gold chain. The days during the Christmas season were joyous ones in the Dunbar house, but the evenings proved nightmarish for Rod. He often found himself jarred awake in the middle of the night, thinking he was still in the jungle. He leaned over to whisper to Grant, knowing the guerrillas would be angry if spoke in loud tones. He whistled, waiting for the kidnappers to turn on a flashlight so he could walk to the latrine in the trees. Each time, it took him a few minutes to realize he wasn't in the jungle any more, that he was home with Jane at his side. He could pad down the hall to the bathroom in his bare feet whenever he wanted.

Rod began to worry about the psychological damage the ordeal had caused. Driving in his Chev pick-up in broad daylight, Rod often had panic attacks, sudden flashes of adrenaline and memory lapses that left him grasping for his intended destination, or the turns he needed to make it home on the once-familiar Edmonton streets. Sometimes he hallucinated, seeing jungle undergrowth in the shade of a snowy cement overpass. He was guarded, less carefree, and had difficulty talking to people—even Jane—about the horrors he'd seen in Ecuador. Speaking to the other men, Rod discovered that he wasn't the only one having problems.

United Pipeline, recognizing the workers had been emotionally damaged, flew the men and their families to a retreat in Arizona where they received medical and psychological treatment from experts in tropical medicine and post-traumatic stress disorders. In between the counselling sessions, some of the men tried to get their minds off Ecuador with rounds of golf. Rod took a Harley-Davidson motorcycle Rob Mackie had rented for a spin through the rounded, burnt-amber hills outside Tucson.

Aftermath   Rod and Jane spoke to one therapist about how the ordeal might affect their marriage. Jane cried as she explained how guilty she felt enjoying the luxuries of life while Rod slept on the jungle floor and ate rotten food. He regretted working away from home so much, neglecting his family for the sake of money. He talked about the long conversations he and Colin had shared in the jungle and how the experience made him value his family more than his job. It was a difficult, but necessary, session.

Rod was skeptical about another event the retreat's organizers had arranged, a sweat lodge ceremony held by a Native American couple, designed to relieve the hostages of the intense anger they felt at being held captive. But Leonard endorsed it, so Rod agreed to try it.

The sweat lodge was a hut made of branches and blankets resembling an igloo. Before entering, Rod was told to strip down to his shorts and take off all his jewellery—the gold chain he wore around his neck, the wedding gift from Jane, might actually scald his skin inside the lodge.

One by one, the hostages walked into the hut. A native elder told the men to turn left upon entering the structure and circle around its interior before sitting. The elder had ventured into the mountains to find special healing rocks for the ceremony; the rocks had been warming in the fire for two days.

The elder chanted and sang about his own life. He said he'd been abused in foster homes and had turned to alcohol to cope with his rage. But before he totally destroyed himself, he decided to turn to the old Indian ways and they had changed his life.

Then the elder sprayed the flames with water, and the lodge was instantly sweltering. The humidity and heat reminded Rod of lying in his hammock in the jungle under the equatorial sun. His body beaded with sweat, and the elder sprayed him with the water to cool him off. The elder and his wife continued chanting and singing, telling the men it was possible to sweat out their anger and fear. He spoke about the wrath the men must feel towards the guerrillas who stole their freedom. Rod found himself in a trance-like state, on the verge of passing out. But the elder told the men to concentrate, to channel their anger and fury into the rocks, that the stones had the power to suck the negative energy out of them.

As the ceremony ended, the elder promised he would bury the rocks and all the evil they now contained, never to be unearthed. The hostages' anger would be gone forever.

Rod wasn't sure his anger would be gone forever, but he walked from the sweat lodge feeling like a load had been lifted from him. He was lighter on his feet and more energetic than he'd been since leaving Fresno for the soul-shattering experience in Ecuador.

During the Arizona retreat, Rod found that the hostages walked a fine line between feeling a euphoric bond over what they had endured, and growing sick to death of each other's faces. By the time it was over, Rod felt he needed a break from the other men and what they'd gone through together. And for a time in early January, he got it.

Only one of the freed hostages, Barry Meyer, returned immediately to work, moving to Durango, Colorado in January to accept the lucrative promotion offered to him before the kidnapping. Despite their conflict in the jungle, Rod wished Barry well. Leonard, too, returned to work in Durango, on Valentine's Day. Meanwhile, Rod's days in Edmonton were filled with appointments with psychologists, magnetic resonance imaging specialists and tropical disease doctors. During one appointment, Rod asked a doctor to examine a painful welt he had under his chin, and the physician cut a five-cm long parasite from the bump. Jane shaved Rod's hair to fight a jungle-borne fungus that was growing in his scalp.

That wasn't the extent of his physical problems, either. Rod's sleeping problems intensified, just as they had in the jungle, and at mealtimes he was either ravenously hungry or unable to eat more than a few mouthfuls. He struggled to put on the thirty pounds he'd lost and stayed for the longest time at a scrawny 150 pounds.

Emotionally, Rod managed to find some relief from a psychologist who performed on him EMDR, or Eye Movement Desensitization Reprocessing. The doctor believed the technique would unlock the traumatic memories of his time in the jungle and diminish their power over him. The technique was commonly used with people who'd witnessed or had been victimized by violent events such as rape, war, or catastrophes such as the Oklahoma City bombing.

During the EMDR sessions, Rod watched his therapist move her finger back and forth in front of his eyes until he drifted into a semi-conscious state. She told him to concentrate on a time from his past when he was totally relaxed. He chose to focus on the days when Krissy was a tiny baby, holding onto his thumb. The therapist then guided him through the terror of the capture, the dread and horror he felt when the guerrillas burst from the trees and stuck a machine gun to his head. She took him through his sickness, through the moments when his temperature soared and he believed he wouldn't wake up in the morning. She eased him into recalling the times he wanted to run and the helplessness he felt watching Barney deteriorate before his eyes.

Before the capture, Rod might have thought techniques such as EMDR were a load of crap, psycho-babble designed to make money off needy people. But after a few sessions of his own, he swore it was working. He could talk about the scariest moments of his 100-day ordeal without that wrenching feeling in his stomach. He could share with Jane more of what he'd gone through, and she could understand why he seemed less carefree now than before the capture.

As if he didn't have enough to worry about, Rod received a letter from United on the first of February that drove him into a rage. United had continued to pay him his regular salary through January. He would have to receive written permission from a psychologist and doctor before returning to work. But the letter he opened on February 1 informed him he would be removed from the payroll immediately, and advised him to seek benefits from Alberta's Workers Compensation Board for the anguish or physical ailments he had suffered in the jungle. Rod stared at the letter with disbelief. After all he had been through, it was unbelievable that United would turn its back on him now. He was grateful that United, or their insurance company, had paid the ransom and saved his life. But now that he was getting his life back together, why was United walking away?

WCB was not a reasonable option. Their maximum payouts paled in comparison to his $2,000-plus weekly salary. He thought of the years he'd spent abroad or in the northern Alberta bush working for United, how he had missed Krissy's first steps and her first words. *This is the thanks I get.*

Rod called Barney and Colin, and discovered that all the Canadians had received similar notes. They were all off the payroll.

Rod steamed, privately blaming United for not providing enough security for the workers on the job. If the company had responded adequately to the concerns brought up at The Block safety meeting two days before the capture, the whole mess would never have happened.

The next day, Rod, Neil, Grant, Barney, Colin and Skunk hired an Edmonton lawyer to investigate the possibility of suing the company for damages. Rod did several media interviews expressing his disappointment with United's position. United fought back equally hard in the press. Ken Foster argued that some of the men would be able to complement their WCB benefits with money from private insurance plans.

"We did not abandon the guys when they were down in Ecuador and we're not abandoning them today," he said. "We want to see the guys come back to work as quickly as they can but only when they're medically fit to do so."

The back-and-forth continued in the papers until early March, when the hostages' lawyer reached a deal with United. Each of them would receive a $75,000 payout from the company as compensation for the time they'd spent in the jungle. In return, United would accept no blame for the incident, and the men agreed not to speak negatively about the company to the media.

The money came as a huge relief to Rod, who was able to continue guilt-free with his appointments and his healing. He treated himself to a new snowmobile and made the renovations to the house he'd planned so carefully while in the jungle. He was still haunted by the kidnapping, but with every board he cut and every fender he painted, his life returned that much closer to normal.

Barney also was trying to guide his life back to the way it once was, but was having difficulty. He struggled to adjust after returning to Edmonton, broke up with his girlfriend and battled through stretches of unrelenting depression. Once he was strong enough to lift the front end of a Volkswagen Scirocco out of a snowbank; now he had trouble hoisting the Christmas turkey out of the oven. Like Rod, he experienced hallucinations that transported him back to the jungle. He would turn a corner in a mall and swivel his head to see a guerrilla brandishing a machine gun or Chemaisu swinging his machete. He'd blink the vision away, but not before breaking into a cold sweat.

One evening at his home, he fractured a knuckle on his right hand by smashing a CD jewel case lying on the floor because he thought he saw ants in the plastic's reflection. Barney told everyone except his former co-workers on the Ecuador pipeline that he'd hurt his hand falling downstairs. But he would look down at his cast and wince at the painful truth.

He thought back to his most despairing times in the jungle, when Rod teased that he belonged in the rubber room. He wondered now if it wasn't true. The nightmares alone might give a psychologist grounds to commit him, he thought. One of the most vivid involved the clean-up crew. In the dream, just as in the one involving his empty coffin, Barney floated above the action, a detached spectator. He watched himself asleep in his hammock, and then looked at the other men dozing in their hammocks, visions of their impending homecoming dancing in their heads. Suddenly, the tall, lean clean-up crew leader snuck into the tarpaulin shelter and shot the hostages in the head one after another, blood splattering on the canvas. Barney shrieked, "Why? Why? Why are you doing this to us?" But the guard couldn't hear him. Then the guard turned the gun on Barney, and he watched his own body buckle with the bullets' impact, shudder a few times, gasp for air, and die.

Awake, Barney was obsessed with vengeful fantasies, ways of paying back the guerrillas for stealing his freedom and pushing him so close to death. In his favourite daydream scenario, he returned to Ecuador, this time as a well-armed mercenary, and kidnapped all fifteen guerrillas. At gunpoint, he forced them onto a plane and ordered the pilot to fly to a remote spot in the Alberta Rockies. Together with the other pipeliners, Barney would hold the guerrillas hostage, forcing them to walk night and day up and down the icefields, beside crevasses and sheer rock faces. He stuck a machine gun in their faces and forced them to eat meagre portions of raw deer meat and mosquito larvae. Knowing how susceptible the South Americans were to cold, Barney would make the guerrillas sleep in next to nothing. He even pissed outside their tent.

Often, the fantasy ended with the guerrillas dying of consumption. But sometimes, they just laughed and soaked in the scenery. Barney was never sure which ending was worse.

But slowly, Barney managed to push his life back on track, returning to work part-time at United in March, travelling northern Alberta taking promotional pictures for the company with the same digital camera confiscated and then returned by the guerrillas. While he felt satisfaction at being of some use again, Barney made a conscious effort to cast his job lower on his list of life priorities. He, like Rod, felt he'd given up too much for the sake of money. He chastised himself for the insane hours he'd worked in the oilpatch before going to Ecuador. He had grown overweight before the South American trip; his body was screaming at him to slow down. Now he was going to start listening.

He found his dances with death in the jungle had made him re-evaluate his life. He could take pride and draw strength from what he'd endured in Ecuador. He'd strayed dangerously close to the edge, both physically and emotionally, but with the help of the other men, especially Rod, he had not fallen over.

One day, Barney even stumbled upon the realization that might one day put his mind totally at peace. Someone asked him, half-jokingly, if he had plans to return to Ecuador. "Hell, no," he said. "I'm never leaving Canada again." But it dawned on him later that the guerrillas—Commandant, Chemaisu, Vladimir, even Mrs. Tiger Tooth—still had a piece of him in Ecuador. To get it back, he thought, he'd have to return to the Oriente, to the dusty gravel highway between Lago Agrio and Tarapoa, and walk that pipeline again, kilometres one through twenty-three.

But this time he'd walk it as a free man, staring daggers into the swaying, jade-green jungle and return to Canada whole again.

Rod, on the other hand, didn't know if he'd ever be over Ecuador. After being released, he and Barney joked it was a shame they weren't freed after ninety-nine days; they wanted tattoos saying "99 days in '99" set against the yellow, blue and red backdrop of Ecuador's flag. Now, Rod was glad he didn't have the tattoo. He thought about what had happened enough without having a constant reminder peeking out from under his shirt.

Because of the EMDR sessions, he could dispassionately recount even the most grotesque details about the kidnapping, as if he were reading them from a script. But he was constantly grappling with his conflicted feelings about the ordeal. The way he had dealt with the other guys, for instance, consumed him. He was proud there was something ingrained in his character that pushed him to stay strong for Barney, Grant and Skunk. But he felt guilty for lashing out at Barry early in the kidnapping. Part of him figured that Barry had reaped what he'd sowed in the jungle, that his boss had all that hostility coming to him. But Rod also felt sorry for Barry. Although his boss was ten years older than the rest of the workers and in a position of authority, he was just as helpless and terrified as they were. He'd dealt with the pressure in his own way and Rod sometimes felt he'd condemned his boss too harshly.

Rod was also bewildered at how his feelings for the guerrillas had modified during his time under their armed watch. At first, he was constantly terrified that they were going to kill him. But then, he grew to depend on them for food and shelter like a newborn relies on its parents. In the end, he saw them as men—violent, single-minded men driven by greed, but men just the same. Was Lario a monster, or just a guy who, like Rod, was trying to make a better life for his family?

He remembered Lario leaving the final encampment without saying a word, remembered Chemaisu's eyes filling with tears on the final day, and saw them as men who were sorry for what they did, men who were genuinely sorry to see their Canadian "friends" go. He almost felt compassion for them, even a grudging respect for what they'd pulled off.

But he didn't know how to rationalize that with the other side of him, the side that wanted to see them all dead—Lario, included—hanged and quartered in some blood-soaked Lago

Agrio square. When Gord Black and two UNASE officers came to Edmonton in February as part of their investigation, Rod happily described the guerrillas to a graphic artist who used a computer to match their features with composite sketches of suspects on disc. He knew his actions might lead to the guerrillas' executions, and he was fine with that.

Rod would find himself standing somewhere and sighing, trying to reconcile those parts of him that were at odds. He worried they always would be.

He did know one thing for sure, at least.

Despite the damage the kidnapping had done, Rod had grown closer than ever to his wife and daughter. Before, it was almost as if they'd lived separate lives under the same roof. But since his return from Ecuador, they talked together all the time. Jane often said it was as if they were on a second honeymoon.

It was strange, but Rod knew his relationship with his family was magically better one day when he was walking down a crowded corridor at West Edmonton Mall with Jane and Krissy. Before his trip to Ecuador, Rod had avoided displays of public affection, and had even preferred to walk four or five steps ahead of Jane when they were out together. But at the mall that day, Rod reached over and took Jane's hand. He noticed his wife's surprised smile, and grinned back at her.

A moment later, Krissy came up from behind, and broke between them, grabbing their hands in hers. They walked that way for a long time and Rod kept smiling, soaking up the mall's bright light and the crowd's frantic energy. His heart swelled with two emotions, one familiar and another he'd taken for granted for thirty-six years.

One was love.

The other was freedom.

EpiLoguE

THE FIFTEEN GUERRILLAS who kidnapped the United pipeline workers in northwestern Ecuador have not been caught, and their identities remain as mysterious as their strange, silent appearance from the jungle. Most people familiar with the kidnapping hold one of two theories about the guerrillas: Either the abductors belong to FARC, the Colombian Marxist army who have steadfastly maintained their innocence, or they are common, well-organized bandits with no political affiliation. Mountie Gord Black, who has been promoted to Inspector of the RCMP's Surrey detachment, shares the latter view. During the Ackerman Group's ham-radio negotiations with the guerrillas, Gord did not once hear them state any concern for the welfare of their fellow countrymen or for the environment. He believes the kidnapping was a self-centred criminal act carried out by mercenaries motivated not by ideology, but by greed.

In the late spring of 2000, though, a third possibility regarding the kidnappers' identities has emerged. Ecuadorean newspapers have begun to report on the existence and activities of a nascent guerrilla group called FARE, or, in English, the Revolutionary Armed Forces of Ecuador. The newspapers report that FARE is a local offshoot of FARC, with leaders imported from Colombia and referred to by the organization's rank-and-file as "Commandant." Considering FARC's unusually vehement denial—they have often happily taken credit for their many "detentions"—and given that the men who took the United pipeliners were so well organized and enjoyed an abundance of local support in Sucumbios province during the kidnapping, it appears that the upstart FARE is a plausible suspect.

The hostages are still dealing with the horrors they experienced in the jungle. Many still attend therapy sessions and most refuse to speak publicly about what they endured, either because they are traumatized and have no wish to relive their time in Ecuador, or because they want to live their lives free of the intrusions of newspapers and television stations.

All of the men appear to have made full physical recoveries from their respective ordeals, however, and, at the time of going to press, had returned to work at United Pipeline Systems' offices in Edmonton and Durango, Colorado. Rod Dunbar is mulling an offer from United Pipeline Systems management to take a six-month contract in Durango. Several of the hostages—Brant "Barney" Scheelar, Colin Fraser, Leonard Carter—grew confident enough to travel immediately and criss-crossed North America on various pipeline-repair jobs.

None have left the comforts and familiarity of North America, however, and it is certain that none of the workers will ever again accept a "routine assignment" in Ecuador.